Unsinkable Spirit

One Man's Journey that Changed the Lives of Thousands of Children

Fred Engh

Headline Books, Inc.
Terra Alta, WV

Unsinkable Spirit

by Fred Engh

copyright ©2015 Fred Engh

To order additional copies of this book or for book publishing information, or to contact the author:

Headline Books, Inc.
P.O. Box 52
Terra Alta, WV 26764
www.headlinebooks.com
www.NAYS.org

Tel: 800-570-5951
Email: mybook@headlinebooks.com

Cover concept credit: Brent Cashman

ISBN 13: 978-1-882658-27-5

Library of Congress Control Number: 2015939491

PRINTED IN THE UNITED STATES OF AMERICA

Dedication

I'm deeply indebted to so many, whose actions, ideas, and help have made this book and the story of our programs for children possible. How to dedicate this book properly to each of them, and give them the thanks they so richly have earned, has turned out to be my toughest challenge of all.

First of all, I dedicate this book to my wife Michaele. She has stood by me throughout all these years, holding things together for us, and without her support there simply wouldn't be a book, let alone the story it tells.

And our seven children—this book is dedicated to them, too. They've created the adventures and life of our family—they all turned out to be great kids and are now successful adults.

Then there are those folks who created miracles giving life to our dreams for children in sports. Like the guy who called and told me to put our training program on video and the neighbor who made it possible by allowing me to use the video equipment at his vo-tech school. Then there's our very first board member who went to the bank with me and protected me from despair when we were stood up for a promised $20,000 in startup money.

And speaking of board members, how can I name every one of them over these past 30-some years, who have guided me and our organization, all on their free time?

And what about back in the very beginning, at the pivotal moment of truth, the three sporting goods company presidents who at the 11th hour provided $36,000 to see that our program got started?

It's scary, sitting here writing this to know I can't possibly do justice to everyone in this limited space. I want no one forgotten because I remember every single person who has taken part in the course of this great adventure.

So the bottom line is, I want to dedicate this book, and express a heartfelt THANK YOU, to all of you who have had a role in making it possible for thousands of children around the world experience fun, better days, in many instances a better life and faith in themselves, through the power of sports.

A special thank you to Dave

A couple years ago, at the urging of my daughter Joanna, I decided to write my memoir. Part of the appeal was the idea that maybe in the way-distant future, if one of my descendants said, "I wonder what life was like back at the time of my great, great grandfather?" they would have an answer. It was fun and redefining to pull together the magical (and not-so-magical) milestones and moments that helped determine the course of my life, and I wish for everyone the unforgettable experience of writing their own memoir for their future generations to read. But on to Dave.

Dave is my son. Sitting at the table, after reading the first two chapters of the memoir I'd started with, he pronounced, "I'd like to have the chance to tell the real story, in a more readable way." I wasn't sure just what he meant, but I got the drift that he wasn't very fond of my writing skills. Since he'd graduated from the University of Florida with a degree in journalism, I had to take his comment seriously, but I thought to myself, *Maybe someday, but not now*. I just wanted to keep writing in my own enthusiastic way and so I continued on writing. When finished, I printed the manuscript myself and gave it to my family and friends. But then the day came that a father finds his kids are smarter than he is, especially when it comes to journalism.

Dave convinced me to write the book you're now holding and tell a story he said needed to be told, and told in a way that the reader will feel inspiration and motivation to never give in to defeat.

We started one summer evening at the dining room table. Page by page he guided me like a ship captain taking an ocean liner through the Panama Canal. With patience and tenacity he demanded I reach deep and pull up every detail that brought the stories to life, spun with storytelling momentum. We laid ourselves open to having more battles than fathers and sons usually have to cope with, to where Dave worried on many nights the experience might ruin our relationship. But always, we ended every night on a positive note.

Never have I been more proud than when the publisher of this book told me when they read the manuscript, they chose to publish it because of the inspirational message and the way the story was told. David had a mindset for how this book should be written and he got his message through loud and clear. For that I am forever grateful.

Foreword

Fred Engh's life could never be made into a movie because no one would ever believe the story.

I have known Fred for the past thirty years and grew to admire him as I volunteered to serve as the attorney for his fledgling nonprofit organization in the early 1980s.

How many people do you know who would leave a secure job with a wife and seven children in the middle of one of the nation's most severe recession? He did so because he hated seeing the abuse thousands of children faced by parents and volunteers who coach in organized youth sports. He did so because he wanted to put an end to these abuses he details in his first book published in 2002 called, *Why Johnny Hates Sports.*

This book is different. It is an inspirational memoir about what led Fred to develop an amazing passion to help children experience the many benefits one can gain through sports. You will marvel at how he overcame many obstacles in his early life, such as having to live in twelve different homes before the age of thirteen or being the first white student at an all-black college only to go on being named to the school's Hall of Fame.

I assure you won't want to put this book down as it will show you that in your own life if you believe, can achieve!

—Rick Robinson,
International Award Winning Author

Introduction

I was sitting at my desk at the office when I received a call from the athletic director of the University of Maryland Eastern Shore. He said, "Fred, this is Keith Davidson and I'm happy to tell you that you have been named a member of the school's Hall of Fame Class of 2012."

I was stunned!

"Simply amazing," I said to myself.

It took me a little while before I fully digested what an honor it was to be included in the company of so many successful people. I would forever be in the books with some of the greatest athletes of all time. My picture would be up in the field house alongside the likes of NFL Hall of Famer, Art Shell, and the football player turned movie actor Fred "The Hammer" Williamson, just to name a couple. But, there was also something awkward and unique about this honor.

When I went to what was then named Maryland State College, I don't remember seeing another white person until my second year at school there. Yes, I'd broken the color barrier by being the very first white person to play on one of the college's athletic teams when I joined the golf team, and we did win the Conference one year, but was that enough to warrant my inclusion in the Hall of Fame, I wondered. I wasn't the greatest golfer in the world and really joined just to be able to play a sport I loved for free. Why did I get selected?

They must have researched and found that I'd created the National Alliance for Youth Sports, an organization with more than a hundred thousand members and that for thirty plus years has had a mission to make youth sports better for kids in a variety of ways.

Maybe someone from the selection committee saw me on television or heard me on the radio through the years while I talked about the need to rid youth sports programs of the evils of win-at-all-cost coaches or parents who abuse their children for not living up to their expectations out on the playing field.

Did they know of my struggles as a child…that I had to put dogs to death at a Humane Society just to help my family have a place to live? Or had they heard that my wife and I lived in a trailer park raising three kids as I traveled back and forth for classes? Or maybe they even knew that, with seven kids to feed, I gambled everything and won when I created my now internationally known organization.

However they determined I was worthy of the honor, I swelled with pride and was on cloud nine. I wanted to tell everyone I knew, especially the many who thought I'd never make it to graduation, let alone be named to the school's Hall of Fame. I wasn't going to miss this for the world.

On the night of the induction ceremony, sitting on the dais with the other inductees, I peered out into the audience of mostly African Americans to see the proud looks on the faces of my now grown children sitting there with my wife, Michaele Anne. While looking at her there, my mind became flooded with memories of how supportive, helpful and positive she had been through the years, both thick and thin. And there were very thin, scary years when we were on the edge of disaster, but she was always there for me.

As I waited for my turn to speak, the words, "I couldn't have made it without you," kept coming to my lips and I sat there with a lump in my throat.

I'd given many speeches in my career, but for some reason had always stumbled when I tried to prepare ahead of time. So I decided to say whatever came to mind after being introduced. Winging it can give you the freedom to relax, but it can also leave you terrified just before you start. Sitting nervously waiting to be introduced, I noticed there was an empty seat next to me. I figured that for one reason or another, one of the inductees didn't show up. But I was wrong, that seat was for Clarence Clemmons, the great saxophonist from Bruce Springsteen's E Street Band. He'd played football at the school around the same time I'd attended, but unfortunately died only a few months before the ceremony. He was inducted posthumously to a standing ovation. I was sure his many amazing contributions to the music world over-shadowed his achievements on the grid iron. In his honor there was a much deserved moment of silence.

Wow, I thought *This is going to be tough to follow!*

The lump in my throat doubled in size, but just then, an idea came to me. After being introduced as the first white athlete to play for this school, I cleared my throat and walked purposefully to the podium and said to this room of more than three hundred people: "It was certainly great to have Clarence Clemons open for me."

The crowd roared with laughter and I was on my way to giving one of the best speeches I'd ever given. I wanted this crowd to know even though I'd had a great time as a student there and was appreciative of what the school provided me, it wasn't a walk in the park. So I told them one of my stories of being on the golf team.

"In 1963, if you were a white guy sitting in a car with five black guys, you were risking more than just angry stares from people. That's in the daytime. At night, forget about it! So you can imagine what it was like riding to golf matches with five black golfers who were like brothers to me. I'd hear the words 'darkie lover' or worse at gas stations and other places we'd stop along the way. It was a two-way street however, on the day we played Morgan State, I remember pulling into a parking lot on campus to hear, 'Hey, there's Big Daddy Lipscomb!' Now Big Daddy wasn't called Big Daddy for nothing. He stood about six foot seven and weighed well over three hundred pounds. I was sure glad to be standing next to my best friend on the team, a guy named Bob Taylor, who was no small guy himself at six four and over two hundred and fifty pounds...when Big Daddy said, as he eyed me up and down, 'Who the hell is this white honkey riding with y'all?'"

Fred Speaking to the audience at his being named to the Hall of Fame.

The audience roared at that and I began to close my speech. I thanked the school and the athletic department, and my family and pointed out my wife, thanking her for everything she's meant to me and everything we'd accomplished. As I stood there for one last moment, I looked out on this crowd and with the past shooting by me in an instant, I said, "I want you to know that without this wonderful school and the people who accepted me here, my life would never have been what it has become. I am truly blessed."

1

1943
The Dogs

I was miserable watching my mother stuff the little white pills into the raw hamburger and roll them into balls. I was mad at her as she did it because it was she who made me take them out to the dogs…to feed them the poison pills of meat… to watch and hear them wince and howl as the Phenobarbital would take effect. It was me who had to drag their carcasses to a long pit that was dug about forty yards into the woods beyond our backyard. It was also me who had to feed them, hose them off, clean them up and shovel their waste until it was their turn to die. The stink of dog urine was so thick around their pens that I can still smell it today in my mind more than seventy years later. It gives me a sick punch in the gut today just remembering it.

In the summer of 1943, I was eight years old and America was at war. I knew a lot about the war because when I wasn't cleaning out dog pens, I was walking up and down the boardwalk of Ocean City, Maryland for hours selling the morning and evening editions of the *Baltimore Sun* for a nickel a copy. Through the headlines I'd read and listening to the people as they would snatch the paper from my hand, I could sense the toll this thing was taking on everyone I knew. I also saw the prisoners of war cleaning up the beaches under armed guard and the concrete lookout towers they'd put up so volunteers could watch for enemy submarines off the coast. Servicemen and their families appeared frayed, on edge and distant. Everybody had a stake in this thing, and everybody seemed to feel some sort of loss, but I didn't. It was more of a sporting event to me…and we were the good guys. I remember being asked to pray for them— the men I'd see often walking down the side of the roadway in their uniforms. One Sunday morning, as I hitchhiked my way to the beach for work, I hopped in the back of a pickup truck with a soldier apparently home on leave.

"Going to the beach?" I asked.

The young man gave me a quick fearful double take and then just sat there across from me staring past as if I wasn't even there. The driver of the truck began to sing "God Bless America" and I remember him stopping and turning back to look at us and yelling, "Why ain't you boys singing?"

There seemed to be a strange mix of pride and fear that had a hold on every adult I knew except one—my mother. She was a devout Catholic and proud-to-be-Irish, a woman whose self preservation and belief in "God's will" trumped anything you could read in a newspaper.

In the spring of that year, we, my mother and father, my older brothers Lynn and Rohn, and my sisters Mary Joel and Dona were desperate. We'd just moved to the Eastern Shore of Maryland from Johnstown, Pennsylvania where we were also desperate. It turned out that my father owed a lot of people money back there.

My father sold insurance in the 1920s and into the 1930s. When the Great Depression hit, it made selling insurance about as easy as selling refrigerators to Eskimos. Eventually he ran out of money and with it went our lifestyle. For a while he worked out a scheme so we could keep the basic appliances in the house by buying on credit and when the business would repossess an item he would simply find another company that would sell a new one on credit. Unfortunately, the scam only worked until he ran out of appliance stores to dupe this way. That wasn't his only problem since now the people he'd sold insurance to made claims against their policies and were dunning him for money owed.

I can still remember hearing my mother plead with the men not to take things from the house.

"Think of the children for heaven's sake! I haven't even cleared the icebox yet!" she yelled futilely at them.

She was brought up in a house in one of the better neighborhoods of Johnstown called Westmont. It sat on top of a long ridge overlooking the city that had already suffered through two devastating floods. She was used to having the things that made life a little easier. Her father owned a soda bottling company and did very well in the years of her childhood.

But things were different now. The credit scam had run its course and our house became empty. We had to move on. Despite my mother's pain and embarrassment, she proudly remained silent as we packed to leave the house. It was pitch black on the night we left. My father still had the 1933 Ford he'd bought when he was selling insurance and we were able to pack the car with two adults and five children. My brothers and sisters and I held in our laps a pile of neatly folded clothes bound with twine…everything else we had was in our pockets. Because we were so packed in there, and I was the youngest, my brothers and sisters made me lay up in the space above them that covered the back window. There was just enough room for me to lie down. In the trunk, there were a few small bags and linens neatly packed, but not much else. My mother sat in the front seat clutching her purse, with a sewing kit between her knees. She could hardly contain her shame and anger as the seven of us crammed in the car and drove out of town.

My mother and father hardly spoke during the ride. We had driven for hours before my sister Dona finally got the nerve to ask, "Where are we going?"

For the next few hours, all I heard was my mother berating my father and disagreeing with every destination he proposed.

"Why in God's name would we want to go to the eastern shore of Maryland and especially a place called Ocean City?"

She asked, "Isn't that some kind of beach resort?" she added with a bit of sarcasm.

"Opportunities," my father said.

My father was a soft spoken Swede whose parents immigrated to America a few years before he was born. He became an orphan at twenty-one years old when both his parents died within a week of each other, leaving him nothing and nowhere to live but the local Y.M.C.A.

In conversation he often spoke of vast ideas in very short sentences and when he talked with you, he often seemed to be in simultaneous deep reflection. He had a way of getting right to the heart of an issue, almost always in a vague but self-assured manner.

"What opportunities?" my mother asked.

I'm not sure if his plan was to soften the blow of being torn away from our home, but it worked on me. I was excited to hear we were going to the beach…a place I'd only heard about from the stories of other children I'd known.

"You need a job and we are stopping at the first place that will let you wash a dish, mister," I heard my mother growl.

I can only imagine they didn't see any opportunities along the way to the coast of Maryland. I'm not certain where we stayed on the night we arrived, but I do remember my mother falling ill. The next day she went to the only doctor in town. During the course of her visit she was asked for an address and revealed that we had none. The doctor offered the six of us a one bedroom apartment in the garage behind his home.

My father had told my mother he had some prospects in the area, but after a week or so looking for work he disappeared. My brother Lynn, who was fifteen, found a way back to Johnstown and lived there with friends. I didn't see him again until he graduated high school. Throughout my childhood, my father would pop in when he'd come across some money, but otherwise he was out on the road trying to find it.

After a month or so living in the converted garage, my mother somehow worked out a deal with a local woman who was tired of running the Humane Society in town. That arrangement gave the five of us a little more space in a small house near Herring Creek in West Ocean City. The catch was that someone would have to take care of the stray dogs, and that person, to my chagrin, was me.

The place actually had what is called a dormer, where on one side I slept with my brother Rohn and on the other, my sisters slept. Somehow we were able to find mattresses to lie on the floor. Rohn was twelve at the time and was off early every day to work any odd job he could find over at the beach, which was a few miles away. It was a long walk, but it was easy to catch a ride hitch-hiking in those days. My sisters were ten and fourteen and had a list of household chores to complete each day.

We were what people called dirt poor and these were times when you never had the time to ask yourself if you wanted to do something—you just did what it took to put food on the table… to contribute...to survive. But even though we were poor, my mother was very proud and worked very hard to keep what we had clean and orderly and I did whatever my mother told me to do. She wouldn't tolerate any emotional negotiating from any of us. We did what we were told to do…that's why. She would simply say, "Dear, we are going to have to make room for three more dogs today."

I knew exactly what that meant. The place had pens for ten dogs, so if three came in…three were getting the little balls of poison burger and a stiff trip to the pit.

I walked out to the pens each morning that summer listening for dogs that might be tied to the loose ropes that were kept on the side of the house. A man from the county would drop them off and tie them there from time to time. I'd know with one glance how many pens I'd need to vacate that day. Mother's rule was that the dogs that were there the longest were the first to go, but on some days, if a mutt seemed nasty or hard to deal with, I used my discretion and fed them their little burger ball without giving them a chance to be adopted, which was pretty rare that summer. I think about forty dogs came in, and only two were adopted.

I'll never forget the very first day I was sent out to do this on my own. Nervously, I carried three little balls of meat covered poison in my hands.

"Here, boy," I said as I tossed one through the bars of the cage with an assuring smile.

The old dog gobbled it up with glee as a trickle of guilt ran up my arm and stung me right in the heart. I did the same thing with the other two dogs that had to be put down. To distract myself from what I'd done, I got busy cleaning up other pens, but I couldn't hide from the sounds the dogs made as they suffered for a few minutes before they died. The barking sounds of the other dogs helped drown out some of the noise and I imagined the chorus of howls and whines was their way of saying good-bye to one of their own.

It took less than a half hour before they staggered over and stopped breathing. No matter how hard I tried to distract myself, it was time for the hard part—touching a dead animal.

On the first day I wanted so badly to rush into the house in tears to inform my mother I just couldn't do it. At that moment, I didn't even think it was possible for me to do it. But I knew what would happen if I went into the house and told her of my fears. She'd march me right back out the door and lock it behind me.

"You'll just have to do it, dear," she'd say.

Like I said, there was no emotional negotiating. It got you nowhere fast with her.

Looking at a dog's corpse wasn't so bad, but the thought of touching the thing was terrifying. So I became resourceful. I found a couple of long sticks and with a piece of rope and invented a tool that allowed me to jiggle a noose around a body part, snag it tight, and then pull the carcass right out of the pen. At first it was slow and clumsy, but with that tool I was able to get them out of their cages and through the backyard to their final resting place.

The pit was a twenty-foot long ditch someone had dug years before. It was the grave of countless dogs and cats and it smelled awful. Looking down on it that first visit made me quickly turn away and dry heave, but I soon found the strength and one by one blindly hurled the dogs down it and ran away.

I have other glimpses of memories from a younger age, but that day was the first day of my life that I knew who I was, or at least, what I did. I was eight years old. I hustled newspapers on the boardwalk for two cents profit per copy, swam in the ocean, played in the woods, and killed dogs for my mother in the backyard.

Levin Jarman was a boy who lived down the road. He was about my age and his family seemed to have even less than we did. His family was from the area and he had the peculiar Eastern Shore accent that sounded like a cross between Tennessee mountain person and English Cockney. My mother hated the thought of any of her children picking it up as she thought it made people sound less educated. I remember the first time he came over to our house he was with my father. My father had been walking home from the road one morning and along the way convinced Levin to come over to play with me. On that day, my father actually spent some time with us throwing an old ball around until my mother called him in. Even though I had a dad who only seemed to visit us, I had it better than Levin. His dad came back from fighting overseas without a leg and some of his hip. Levin told me they were blown off when he'd set off a bomb that killed a thousand Nazis. I never saw his dad in person, but Levin told me many stories of all the Germans he'd killed during the war. He told me his dad, these days, sat all day and night in a dark corner of their living room in a wheelchair drinking whiskey and listening to the radio.

We threw that ball for hours talking on the day we met.

"Yaver been to a game?" Levin asked.

"What kind of game?"

"Ball game, a course."

"Nah," I said.

"Yer shittin' me…me neither. I listen witma day all the time dough…He useta to go see the Yanks when he weres in Na York."

"Wow," I said, trying to sound a little impressed.

"We listen onna radio tall da games."

"Lucky."

"Yeah, weeze gone to a game wheneeze better."

"Lucky."

"Spose to be getting' a new leg…a wood one."

"Wow," I said, trying a little harder to sound impressed.

"Whats yer dad do?" Levin asked as he tossed the ball to me.

"Oh, he sells insurance," I said quickly.

"Yer shittn' me…What's that?"

"Not really sure, but he's gotta be outta town for meetings and stuff."

"Yer shittn' me…Where to?"

"I don't know. Back in Johnstown I think. Listen, my mom hears you cussin'…you won't be allowed around here," I warned.

"Okay… Hey! You see that?" Levin shouted as he ran off to the side of the house.

I could see a chicken flap and dash off as he reached down and grabbed something and raised it into the air. It was a rat. He held it by the tail and smiled a huge smile at me. As he walked toward me with it, I cautiously backed off.

"Waats wrong…ga?" he said as he laughed a little.

Just then the thing swung up in a snap and caught Levin's index finger and chomped down to the bone. He began screaming bloody murder and swinging that thing, but the rat had a good chunk of Levin's finger in its mouth and wouldn't let go. Just then I saw my father bolt out of the house and pick up a board that happened to be lying nearby.

"Set it down!" he hollered at Levin as he pointed to a small bench.

Levin slapped the rat down on it and I could see that the rat had bitten down on his finger with a tight defiant grip. The board came crashing down hard an all I could see was Levin's broken bloody finger dangling off of his hand.

My mother came out of the house with a rag and covered and wrapped up the wound with a disgusted look on her face. I got the feeling that she was more upset about losing a good rag than actually caring about Levin's finger. She sent my dad off to take Levin home with anger on her face as if it were his fault. I didn't see Levin again for about a month. I didn't see my dad again until Christmas that year.

The next time I saw Levin we were thumbing to the beach and caught a ride together. As he showed me the ugly scar on his hand he asked, "Ever seen a Crat?"

I had no idea what he was talking about, so I shrugged.

"Them German son bitches, they got 'em workin' on the beach wit guards round 'em ready to shoot if dey try anythin'."

In the summer of 1943, it was common to see the prisoners of war walking the beaches picking up trash. People would sit and stare from the benches on the boardwalk as if they were animals in a zoo. The beaten-down men, wearing faded grey prison suits under heavy guard, slowly picked up the trash left behind by tourists.

On this day, Levin had convinced me to crawl to a place under the boardwalk where we could get a good close view of these men. The guards never noticed us there as we gawked through the pilings, but one of the prisoners did.

"That's a Crat," Levin whispered.

"Yeah."

The prisoner slowly walked closer to us and began to stare back as we all froze there for a moment. All I could think about was how he looked like so many of the men who had given me rides to the beach or bought papers from me. Then for an instant in the moment, it got uncomfortable. I could see in his face the humility and desperation he felt. Like seeing an animal caught in a trap, my first instinct was to try to help him. He had a look on his face that I'll never forget because it wasn't what I expected. I didn't see a hateful look on his face, all I saw was a sad look of compassion and longing. It took me many years to finally realize what that probably meant—he was thinking of his own children.

After a couple months of work at the backyard Humane Society, I'd taken the Phenobarbital burger balls out to about three dozen dogs. It got easier. By then, I was even touching the dead dog's stiffened limbs to get the noose around them. Most of the dogs that came in were mangy and old, but every once in a while a young pup would get dropped off and I would immediately set them up with the hopes of their quick adoption. I'd make sure that their pens were clean, they were fed well, and do anything I could to make them a little more presentable to somebody who might want to take them home. As you might imagine, it was pretty easy to really hope for some of the dog's adoption, but the reality was if you were here, you were only alive while there was room.

The spot where Fred had to bury the dogs after they were euthanized.

One day the man from the county dropped off a dog I was sure would be adopted. It was small Shepherd mix that looked to be about a year old with a white crooked stripe between black and gold down its back. There was something different about this dog. It seemed to carry itself with a sense of pride or purpose. Any time I would approach its pen, it would behave as if it had known me for a long time. I didn't have to fear being bitten or it trying to run off as I would open the cage door. The dog simply behaved as if it were happy, despite being stuck in our backyard locked in a stinking little pen. After a few weeks though, his number was up. And even though I'd been keeping his pen the cleanest, there were no takers. That was when I started bending the rules and bypassing his cage when I had a burger ball to feed, and before long, it was like having my own pet. I even gave the dog a name. It made the job of killing these things easier knowing that I had the power to save one.

"Dat's Scrap?" Levin asked as we looked through the cage door.

"Yup," I said a little proudly.

"He a good dog," he said as if he could tell right away.

"Yeah."

"Why Scrap?"

"'Cause he looks like he can."

"Waat? Fieght?"

"Yeah. He looks like he could scrap if he had to."

"I bettys in hundrits of fights for he got here," Levin agreed. "He ain't mean dough."

"He's not. He's just a good dog."

"Yep he'd whoop these sad dogs," Levin pointed down the row. "Ever a dog and one doze cats aver scrap?"

"No, cats just bunch up and hiss and the dogs never do anything."

"Ya gonna teach 'em tricks 'n stuff?"

"No, I'm not really allowed to play with him."

Levin then lowered his voice to a whisper and said, "Your momsa a b-i-t-c-itch, I tail ya."

"Yeah, well, she'll be out here grabbing your ear if she hears you."

"I know, hey, what if we took 'em in da woods and kep him there down by the fert. He cud be da guard dog."

We'd nailed some boards together in a tree a few hundred yards into the woods beyond the property. Levin had shown up a few weeks earlier with some broken down boxes and a bag of nails he'd stolen from a construction site nearby and it wasn't long before we had a place to call, "The Fort." My mother knew nothing of it.

I can still remember daydreaming about what Levin had said. I'd think, *Why not?* I could keep him there tied to our tree. It would have to be better than being in that cage all day. We could feed him out there, play with him, even build him his own little dog house out there. It all sounded good in my head until I thought of my mother. I certainly knew I could never ask her if I could keep a dog in the woods…in a fort she knew nothing about. It was just a dream that would play out in my head, but in my heart I knew it could never really happen.

On one beastly hot August day, Levin came by and said, "Hey, wanna go outin' see the herses runnin?"

I'd finished everything I had to do in the backyard that day and my mother wasn't home so I said, "Yeah," with relief.

He convinced me to bring Scrap along on a short rope and as we walked through the woods we tried to teach the dog to sit and stay. Remarkably, the dog obeyed our every command and we laughed in amazement. The Riddle Farm was one of the most successful and famous horse farms in the country. It was where the popular champion race horse, Man 'O War, was trained. How we ended up living only a mile or two from it was a complete coincidence.

As we approached it, we looked for a place we could hunker down behind the trees to get a good view of the horses as they trotted by. We knew if we were spotted we'd be run off in a heartbeat by the stable workers there. I gently pet Scrap to calm him down for fear he'd bark, but he seemed to instinctively know to keep quiet.

"Dat's a fassest herse I ever sane," Levin said.

"Yeah pretty fast…how do those guys hang on like that?"

"Dey trainen. Dat's what dey do all day, everday. That's how come they has so many champs," Levin informed me.

These were some of the fastest and most beautiful things I'd ever seen. Their color, their power and precision as they ran, was overwhelming.

But just then, it happened. Scrap began to bark at an approaching horse…it was spooked and almost threw the rider. We had to run for it—as far and fast as we could. After tearing through the woods for about ten minutes, we had to stop just to breathe.

The summer heat made it hard to catch my breath and I knew it had to feel the same to Levin and Scrap. We had to search for a creek or something to get some water as soon as we could. Scrap began to walk in a direction and just pulled me behind with Levin following.

"Dat ain't the way back," he yelled.

But in a matter of minutes we all sat in a creek together drinking it in through every pore.

"Datta a smartass dog there, boy!" Levin smiled as he lay there soaked from head to toe.

On the way back to the house we talked to and about Scrap as if he were our new best friend.

"You think you could keep him at your house?" I asked Levin.

"Why not jus' keep 'em at the fert?"

"That won't work. Someone'll find him out there, or my mom'll hear him. It won't work," I said with a sad certainty.

"I'll ask, but I ownt thint so.…You sher a smartass dog, Scrap!" he said as he looked down at him.

I swear that dog looked like he understood and agreed with every word.

The summer passed and left me with many early memories: the smell of Thrasher's fries cooking on the boardwalk, the taste of Fischer's sweet popcorn, the burn of hot sand on my feet and the vastness of the ocean at sunrise, to name a few. But the long days of exploring in the woods and playing in the sand were over too soon and it wasn't long before I was sitting miserably in a classroom on a hot September afternoon feeling like a dog in a cage.

One day walking home from the bus stop, I was passed by the man from the county in his truck. He gave me a wave, but hardly looked at me. When I got home I could see them there, it looked like as many as ten dogs were tied there on the side of the house. Then I looked to the back of the house where I could see my mother standing and my chest began tighten. As I walked toward her, I saw the sight that I'd feared to see—she held a little empty pan out and said, "I've fed them… I thought I'd get you started…there's so many."

I ran into the house trying not to let her see me crying. I knew what I had to do, but couldn't imagine being around them now knowing they'd been fed...knowing Scrap had been fed. I sat up in my room with my hands over my face until I heard my mother come in the back door. I knew what that meant. I knew I couldn't hide in my room anymore and what I had to do.

On this day, I didn't even bother to use my tool. One by one, I bit my tongue and gritted my teeth and dragged their stiff bodies by hand and threw each one in to the pit. After nine in a row, I walked back for the last one, Scrap. While I did it, my eyes began to well up with tears and I could feel my mother watching, whether she was or not. It began to rain and I felt my insides begin to pour out and wail. Tears were falling as I picked up the mutt in my arms and made my way to the big hole in the ground. The dirt around it had become mud as I approached and I looked with resentment over at the bunch of new dogs there on there ropes.

For the first time, I gave this nasty pit a good long look and spat down into it. Half buried carcasses and bones were everywhere, not to mention the nine fresh ones. Then with an angry strength I didn't know I had, I hurled Scrap into the air with all my might and let out a howl of my own as my feet slipped from the edge. I was falling, too. My body twisted as I fell and before I knew it, my back hit splat on top of the dogs. I remember laying there for an instant looking up at the rain as it fell down on my face and wondering, *Am I alive?*

At that moment, I wasn't sure that I wanted to be, but as the putrid air wrapped around my face and shot up my nostrils and into my mouth, I sprang up and feverishly began to claw at the dirt on the side of the pit. I was terrified as my feet squished into the soft bony dog decay below me. I never thought of screaming for help, but I still remember how I whimpered and cried as I desperately tried to make my escape. There were roots and rocks that I grabbed hold of and within seconds I was half way up the wall with my feet sticking into the sides but slipping. It seemed at that moment like I was making the sharpest and most critical decisions I'd ever have to make—which root to grab and what rock to trust as I did anything and everything to progress up and out of this mess. Everything I did to keep from falling back into that stink and mush below had to be right. One slip or snatch of the wrong rock meant I was falling back down into the gore. I couldn't let it happen. After a good five minutes of careful climbing and clinging, I carefully reached a piece of sod that was at the top. With that in grip, I was able to quickly hoist my hips and fluttering feet over to the wet grass and I lay there in the rain not believing what had happened.

I first thought of my mother, then my brothers and sisters, then my father, and for the first time how truly alone I was in this world.

I eventually got up, put the new dogs into their pens, hosed myself off and went into the house. The next morning I sat in the kitchen with a blanket around me shaking uncontrollably trying to hold on to a salty cup of chicken broth with both hands. I'd woken in the middle of the night with a terrible fever that lasted for about a week. My mother fretted over me seemingly every second with cold rags for my head and plenty of hot broth.

When the fever finally did break, I remember peeling off the sweaty blankets with a sense of vigor I'd never had before. I felt like nothing could ever knock me down like that again.

A couple days later I saw Levin at school and gave him the bad news about Scrap. He also became the first and only person I ever told about falling into the pit.

"From da tap? All da dam way down init?" he asked smiling and full of excitement.

"Yup."

"You gotta be shittin' me!"

2

1948
Johnstown

After five years of struggling just to make ends meet there on the Eastern shore, my mother thought it would be best for us to return to Johnstown. The schools in Ocean City and nearby Berlin didn't offer the kind of education she thought would help us achieve in life. I also think she yearned to return to her roots. My brother Lynn was already there. Rohn and Mary Joel had moved to Baltimore. He was studying at an Art School and she was there earning her room and board at a Catholic high school by working at a convent. So it was only my sister Dona and I with our one-year-old baby brother Denis who were being packed up and put in the old car for the trip back to what our mother called home. We hadn't seen our father in months.

I remember how upset my sister was about leaving and I was too, but neither of us made a peep about having to leave. We knew better than to complain. For the first time, my mother seemed fragile to me. She was on edge and very determined, but I can also remember hearing her murmur how defeated she felt on the day we were packing.

"Go outside and find something to do!" she said in a panicked voice.

"Why?" I asked.

Then she said to my astonishment, "Because I think I'm going to die."

I remember going outside and just standing and wondering, *What did she mean?* and what I would see when I finally got the nerve to return to the inside of the house. *Why would she say something like that to me?* I wondered. I'd never heard her this way before.

After about an hour, I walked back on to the porch and slowly opened the kitchen door. There she stood, as if nothing had happened at all. I walked out of the room and went straight for the car and waited alone.

It was time for a change and like our original trip out of Johnstown, we were moving on with not much more than the clothes on our backs and the few things we could carry.

By 1948 things were a lot different on the Eastern shore. I'd seen drastic changes in the people and the place in the last five years. We'd dropped the "Big One" and soldiers were coming home. I still remember selling that morning edition of the *Sun* paper with the headline: "WAR IS OVER," a few weeks later. We won. People in the area walked and talked with a little more confidence and pride. They'd stopped putting the prisoners on the beach and there was no more need for volunteers to sit in those concrete towers. The people were more excited to watch something else now—television. They had them in lobbies of some of the hotels off the boardwalk and they always seemed to attract a crowd. I'll never forget the awe I felt looking at the round screen with moving pictures of people talking in black and white. You could actually see them as they talked! You could see the ball game while it was being played up in Philadelphia or New York. It was stunning to see this for the first time and I dreamed of being able to have one to watch baseball someday, but of course it was the last thing my family could think of ever owning.

That summer, like the summers before, I spent most of my time there at the beach. When I wasn't selling papers, I was in the ocean or playing with friends in the sand. I also had a job making ten cents an hour setting pins by hand at a bowling alley off the boardwalk. For hours, my buddies and I would dash from lane to lane setting and resetting the pins back on the hardwood as the balls would swoosh by and whack the thick tarp. I wasn't making a lot of money, but I never got hungry. The best food in the world was only steps away out there on the boardwalk. I'll never forget how my friends and I would sit around after a long day eating fries and hot dogs. I had no complaints about my life at the time, but if Mother said we had to move, we had to move.

My grandfather, who had fallen on hard times, had offered to move out of his small apartment and leave it for us. My mother explained to me on the trip how he'd lost everything at the bottling company and now he worked in a building downtown. I was twelve years old and thought I'd seen a lot to this point, but I didn't know this was going to be one the toughest years of my life.

On the day we returned, my mother pulled the old car up to a building downtown and asked my sister to wait in the car to watch after Denis while she and I went inside the building. She was talking to people in the lobby when I spotted the elevator and immediately walked toward it. I'd been on one before back in Ocean City and couldn't resist hoping aboard for a quick ride. But as I did, I was filled with a mix of confusion and dread as I laid eyes on the man in the grey vest. He was looking the other way and I immediately ducked and cowered in the back behind a man with a large briefcase. I wondered if he would recognize me…it had been seven years since seeing him last, but my mother had a picture of him on the kitchen wall that I'd spent many mornings staring at it as I ate my breakfast. It was a grainy photo of him standing in front of a desk…arms folded with a big cigar in his hand and a confident look on his face.

I watched him through the openings between the people in this crowded elevator and caught a glimpse of his matching vest and hat. He was sitting on a small bench maneuvering the arms of the elevator doors. The people barked their floor numbers at him and I watched him sigh as he pulled the cage-like doors to a locked position and cranked in the numbers.

He was my grandfather. The same man my mother had taken me to visit seven years earlier when we still lived here. I remembered her proudly walking with me into the huge bottling company, down the carpeted hallway and into his office of dark green walls. My grandfather, who was smoking a cigar and reclining in his chair at the time, shot up with excitement when he saw us. He took us to a fancy restaurant downtown where I can remember asking about the ice cream on the table. He said, "No, that isn't ice cream…that's butter."

I'd never seen a scoop of butter laid out in a bowl like that before. In those days my grandfather was doing very well, but it wasn't long after that day that the fragile economy that followed the Great Depression took its toll on his business. Unfortunately, in a matter of a few short weeks in 1940, he went from making a lot of money to owing a lot of money.

"Maybe I'm wrong," I said to myself trying to fool myself. "Maybe this man isn't my grandfather."

But it was, and I knew it every time I got a glimpse of any part of his body. It was only a matter of time before the elevator would be empty and my cover would be gone. *What would I say to him?*

The anguish I felt at the moment overcame me and as the next group walked off I made my escape. I scurried and sidled up next to a man as he walked off. I was three or four steps clear of the thing when something overtook me and forced me to look back, and there he was…staring…eye to eye…with a lost look on his face. Cringing with confusion, I didn't know what to do, so I did the first thing I thought of—I turned and walked away. I could hear the doors sliding and locking shut and felt some relief, but my heart felt terribly wrong. Then it dawned on me that I would still have to face him down in the lobby with my mother.

I walked the stairs down seven floors and as I opened the doors I could see him there talking with her. When she saw me across the room in the doorway, she darted across the floor and grabbed me by the collar and said sternly, "What are you doing, young man?"

She pulled me across the room until I was at my grandfather's feet. He pretended as if it were the first time he laid eyes on me.

"Hey, Freddy! It's time for lunch and I can use a break. Wanna go for lunch?" my grandfather asked with a big smile.

He took us to a diner across the street and as the four of us ate grilled cheese sandwiches, he told my mother how he'd completely moved out and the place was ready for us to move in. When we'd finished eating, my mother took my sister and baby Denis to the bathroom. As my Grandfather and I sat there awkwardly at the table, he asked me if I wanted ice cream. I said no. I certainly didn't feel like I deserved any ice cream… and then he said, "First time on an elevator, Freddy?"

As he spoke, the picture of him on the kitchen wall was hanging before my eyes.

"No, I rode on one back in Ocean City."

"Yer kidding. I hope you liked the ride today!" he said.

His laughter gave me a sense of ease and I smiled and said, "I did."

"Come by any time…we'll do it again."

During the long year we were back in Johnstown, I never did. I wished for the feeling of guilt over the way I'd treated him to go away, but it stayed with me like a scar.

My grandfather moved out of his apartment the day before we got there and the place still smelled of thick cigar smoke. But there was a room for me and my sister to set up a bunk bed and for my mother to sleep on a pull-out sofa with baby brother Denis in the living room.

It wasn't long before I was at a new school and for me, the transition was no picnic. I'd had some troubles learning back at the public school in Ocean City, but here they were magnified by the new teachers who treated me poorly and gave up trying to teach me very early on. On top of that, I was an outsider here, and the inside crowd of 8th grade kids were unwelcoming to put it mildly. Being new, poor, and smaller than a lot of the other kids, I was vulnerable to bullying and abuse by them. A day didn't pass that first month I wasn't made fun of, called stupid, pushed or flicked in the back by somebody's pencil. My books were knocked out of my hands more times than I can remember. That transition made me reclusive and fearful.

"Today at school they had me read out loud," I told my mother.

"Was it hard?" she asked.

"The hard part was that I wasn't the first one to read. I had to go after other kids who could read fast, and when it was my turn I didn't know some of the words and some of the kids laughed…I could hear them."

"Don't worry Freddy, you'll catch on."

I ended up going to the YMCA just around the corner and down the street from where we lived as often as I could. Some days I was there for more than eight hours swimming in the pool, running on the track, or playing basketball in the gym. I remember how exhilarating it felt to leave that small apartment and race down in the gym. I used to play a basketball game by myself for hours there, shooting foul shot after foul shot. I'd run up and down that court making imaginary game winning shots…driving to the hoop and laying it in at the buzzer. The place had a smell that I grew to love. The smell of sports— sweat. It hovered and wafted in the air no matter where you were in this place. The clopping of feet running around the track and the clanging of weights being dropped on mats made me feel alive. I especially liked the sound of the echo in the gym as the basketball met the wooden floor. It was a paradise compared to sitting in that apartment, waiting for my mother to let me leave for the day.

After a month or so I got so good shooting fouls and dashing in for lay-ups, I bragged to my brother Rohn who was in town for a visit.

"Yeah, I'm down at the Y all the time playing basketball," I said.

"So you must be getting pretty good, eh?"

"I made ten foul shots in a row…you know how hard that is?"

"That's great Freddy, are you gonna play on a team?"

"Yeah, try-outs are coming up."

I decided to join a league there after one of the coaches encouraged me to do it. He'd seen how hard I'd worked on my game and told me that I was a pretty talented kid. When I heard that word talented…that phrase—I was talented…something inside me came to life. It made me work even harder to earn respect and to excel.

As practice began in this league, right away I could see two things about the team I was on…I was shorter than most of the other boys and many of them played on the same team the year before. That was okay though—I was "talented." It really didn't take long for me to prove to the other guys on the team that if they gave me the ball, I was going to make something happen with it. Either by scoring or passing to the open man, I was pretty consistent and they knew it.

The coach, however, ignored me. He was focused on the kids who were on the team from the previous year with a lot of prejudice against me, the "new kid with the old sneakers." Even when I'd make a good pass or shot, it was overlooked by this guy. I didn't get discouraged though. It made me work even harder as we scrimmaged.

"You think your gonna be one of the starters?" one of my teammates asked with a knowing smirk on his face in the locker room after a practice.

"I just want to play," I said

"Well you ain't gonna start…that's for sure. Favorites start no matter what…and he's gonna play his son the whole game. That's a fact."

That "fact" didn't really seem to bother me so much because I believed in myself. I believed in the fact I could put a basketball through the hoop and I believed I could out-hustle any one of my teammates one-on-one. For the first time in my life I was on a team and that made me feel so vital. A couple days before our first game, they handed out team uniforms and when I was given a shirt with my own number on the back I swelled with pride.

When it was time for the first game I was so excited to play I asked my brother Rohn, who was still in town, to come watch and he did. He even brought some of his friends. I remember looking up in the stands at all the other kid's parents and was comforted knowing that he'd made time for this. But then the game started and I realized I didn't make the starting line-up. The coach's son, who I thought I was twice as good as me, was the starting point guard. I watched fitfully as we fell behind by ten points very quickly and by half time we were down by twenty.

I thought at halftime the coach would tell me I'd get my chance…he'd surely put me in. But as the second half started, I sat there glaring angrily at my coach. My brother patiently waited and I could tell he knew how I was feeling. I sat there and with every tick of the clock I wished that at some point this coach would see me and remember he hadn't given me a chance yet. We were getting clobbered—he would surely give me a shot down the stretch. I looked at my brother up in the stands as time was winding down and then I leaned over to the coach and begged, "Can I play the last few minutes?"

"Not this game…not going to happen…not with those shoes on…now go sit down!"

I remember the tears forming in my eyes. I was devastated, humbled, hurt and embarrassed. He'd not only made me feel insignificant but also humiliated me in front of the others for being poor and that really hurt.

Rohn and his friends sat in the stands for the whole game but disappeared quickly after and I was grateful they did. I'd told Rohn what good player I was and all he saw was a kid not good enough to even get in the game. I could only imagine what he and his friends were thinking as the whole game passed and I didn't even get to play.

I hated my coach for making me feel this way. For making me feel less than the others. I'll never forget how he ignored me there as I sat like a keg of dynamite on the edge of the bench waiting to get my chance. When I went home after the game, I walked pass my mother and baby brother without a word and went straight to my bunk bed. I bunched my team shirt in to a ball on the way home and threw it against the wall. I was happy to see my brother wasn't there to ask me anything about the game. I'm sure he sensed my embarrassment and decided to stay away until the next day so the obvious hurt could dissipate. I'd never felt so powerless, but it taught me one of the most important lessons of my life—I never wanted to be put in a situation where I had such a lack of control ever again.

I quit the team a few weeks after that game and lost interest in practicing basketball all together. It took almost a year before I became interested in a team sport again. But when I found the sport, I knew it was for me. It was a sport that would give me back what had been taken away from me on the basketball court—the control over what I achieved in competition…the sport was WRESTLING.

3

1949
Hell and Heaven

Late in the summer of 1949, only a few days after I'd turned 14, my mother gave me the news. I never had to go back to the public school in Johnstown. By talking with a priest at our local Catholic Church, she'd arranged to have me sponsored to attend a seminary in Baltimore. It was on the condition I would someday return to our parish as a priest. My mother's maiden name was Harrigan and she wore the pride in her heritage and her Irish Catholic faith on her sleeves. I believe it was her dream to have at least one of her sons go into the priesthood and I was the "chosen one"…so she thought. She told me the school was called St. Charles Seminary and it was full of nice boys and I was sure to make many friends there.

I had no idea what a seminary was or what I was in for. My father, who I hadn't seen in months, picked me up on the curb outside our little apartment. For some reason, he'd promised my mother to drive me to the Seminary. As I walked down the sidewalk from our apartment building, he said, "Ready?"

"Yes," I said standing there with a small duffle bag in my hand.

"You have everything you need?" he asked with a casual tone and ease as if we'd spoken about it the day before.

"Yes," I said grimly as I tossed the bag into the car.

Where Fred went to a seminary at his mother's urging.

I could only sit there in the car wondering why this man, who I called my father was doing this. I hadn't seen him in over a year. *Why was he the one taking me to this place?* I wondered.

It was a long drive from Johnstown to Baltimore on two lane highways that lay along side countless farms and hillsides and it left a lot of time for my dad and I to talk, but we had very little to say, having not seen him in a while made it difficult and awkward.

"Why are you taking me to this place?"

"I told your mother I would."

I wanted to ask why he never came to visit us in Johnstown. I wanted to ask him why he didn't live with us like other fathers. I wanted to ask why he didn't want anything to do with me. But I didn't.

"Do you think there will be sports at this place?" I asked.

"Freddy, at this school you will learn about becoming a priest. There aren't sports to play there."

"What do they do for fun?" I asked sadly.

"Freddy, the one thing you have going for you is that people like you. So no matter what you do there, I'm sure you will be happy."

38

Just then I remembered how he told me how I'd like the school back in Ocean City the morning before my first day there. He was wrong about that, but I sure wished I was there instead of going to this strange new place.

"Where have you been?" I asked as I thought of how my brother cried when my father didn't show up for his graduation ceremony from high school.

He explained things were tough and he had to travel for days and weeks at a time looking for work. I shrugged as if I understood and then struggled to think of what else to ask him.

"Still playing pool?" I asked.

I remembered the times when we were younger he'd take me and my brothers and sisters to the movies for a double feature. He'd always tell us to meet him at a nearby pool hall after the shows. Sometimes we'd meet him and he'd be so happy to see us he'd take us for candy. Other times he'd have a disgusted look on his face as if he wished we didn't exist.

"Do I have to go to this place?" I pleaded.

"Do you want to break your mother's heart?"

"No," I said dutifully, but not really meaning it. "I don't want to go to this school," I said fearfully.

"It is all set…your mother is counting on you. You don't want to let her down, do you?"

It felt like we were going a million miles away from anywhere or anything I would like. I wasn't crazy about living in that small apartment we squeezed into in Johnstown and going to that school, but it was home.

For a moment I thought, *Maybe my mother is right…maybe it won't be so bad. It will have to be better than the school back in Johnstown.*

I was wrong though, and knew it the first time I laid eyes and ears on the place. I heard strange male voices chanting eerily as we approached the grey and dark, stone-faced compound that surrounded an ivy-covered chapel in the center. I desperately hoped my father would stop the car…and grab my shoulder and say to me "Freddy, I'm sorry…this place isn't for you." But he didn't. He pulled right up to the stone steps, walked me into the front door and dropped me off as if I was a box being delivered. He signed some papers as I sat in the hallway. This wasn't a school as I knew schools. This place was dark, cold and strangely quiet.

"Everything is going to be fine," my father said unconvincingly as he walked past and out the front door.

I truly felt like a prisoner the moment the doors shut behind me. All the other boys and young men seemed like prisoners, too. I felt threatened and scared as I looked around the place and my heart sunk thinking this is where I was meant to stay. When they showed me the places I was to bunk, to study, to pray, to sing and work I began to cry on the inside. They didn't mention free time at all. Now, all my time was to be the Lord's time.

I didn't fit here and I dreaded the fact I had to stay, but couldn't say a word. It was not long before I was mistreated and bullied by the older boys there. These were supposed to be nice kids who were selected from their communities to someday represent their town's parish and religion. I'm sure a lot of them were good kids, but the ones I met on the first day there were not. Two older boys were assigned to show me around the place.

"What's your name?" one of them asked.

"Freddy," I said.

"You like spaghetti, Freddy?"

"Yes," I said, and noticed we were walking into a large room where there were many boys sitting at tables eating.

"Because you are new here, you'll get to ask for anything you want for lunch…you'll see. It's your special day," the boy explained, and for the first time, I felt a little at ease.

Maybe this place isn't so bad, I thought.

We were in a long line with other boys waiting to get their food and I could see it wasn't spaghetti, but as we got to the man handing out the food, the boys turned to me and said, "Just tell 'em it your first day and you want the spaghetti."

It didn't feel right, but I said, "Can I have the spaghetti?"

The man just smirked at me and handed me a roll and slid me a bowl of what looked like tomato soup. The two boys laughed all the way to the table. As we sat down to eat with the others, I was introduced as Freddy Spaghetti.

Most of these kids, I believe, felt the same as I did inside and hated being there and being subjected to things normal kids would never want to do. Most of the boys slept in a huge room filled with probably fifty small cots and I sadly was afflicted with the worst possible problem a boy can have at that age—I wet the bed. The very first morning there, I woke to the sound of a boy who slept next to me shouting to the room, "Freddy wet the bed."

I was marked now. These kids only needed that one thing to tease and humiliate me. And they did constantly. I silently cried myself to sleep at night with the fear of how I would be teased in the morning. Some days I would even go without water to try to escape from the embarrassment.

Every morning we were required to wake at four in the morning to sing Gregorian chants before breakfast and then long hours of lectures on history, languages and religion. Most nights, I lay fretting over going to sleep so much that I could hardly stay awake during these long and boring classes. I quickly fell behind and my grades were awful.

There was one escape from the harsh realities of my hated life there, and just like back at the YMCA, it was a sport. There was a ping pong table in the small recreation room. It was there, and only there, as I hit a little white ball I felt normal. We were given one hour a day to rest and I used it to play ping pong with anyone who would play with me. I loved to play and was good at it from the first moment I grabbed a paddle. In fact, nobody at this place could beat me. As I was playing one day an older kid walked into the room and demanded the kid I was playing hand over the paddle.

"It's mine!" he said as he swiped it out of the kid's hand. Then he pointed the paddle at me and said, "Heard your pretty good...What's your name?"

"Freddy."

"Freddy that wets the beddy, Freddy?"

Instead of answering, I served him the ball.

"My name's Tom. I brought this paddle from home."

He was a good player and at first I liked the fact he was good because it gave me a challenge, but he wasn't a good sport and I soon ended up losing games on purpose just so he wouldn't have a tantrum after losing. After we'd play, he would follow me and demand my friendship in a very intimidating way. I didn't want to be around this guy at all, but he had a threatening manner that made me feel if I didn't act like a friend, there would be trouble.

The fathers in this priesthood seemed to be in their own world and totally oblivious to how the boys felt. Most of the time, I felt I had no recourse but to obey the bullies and I hated it. Tom would seek me out in the dining hall and sit next to me. He'd quietly tell me how much he hated the place, too. We did have that in common, but I didn't share the anger he seemed to carry with him. I couldn't relate to him. I was intimidated by him and really couldn't do anything about it. All I could think about was how trapped I felt at the seminary and this kid only made it worse. He didn't seem to have any other friends, so because I was afraid he would beat me up, I was his "friend."

The classes were even more difficult for me than at the public school and I had a lot of trouble keeping up with the others. It wasn't long before I was in the Office of the Prefect which was like the principal at the public school being asked about my poor performance.

"What seems to be the problem, young man?"

I wanted to say that I hated everything about this prison, but I just said, "I don't know."

"You have been caught falling asleep in class on many, many occasions. Why do you think that is?"

"I don't know," I repeated.

"Freddy, you are in the Lord's house now and you must be aware he sees all and knows all. You want to try harder for the Lord, don't you?"

"Yes," I responded.

"Then we are going to get you some help."

I didn't need help; I needed to get out of that place. They had another student tutor me for a while and he was a nice person, but I could tell he wasn't entirely happy to be there either.

He was like so many of the other boys there—brainwashed into thinking obeying would bring you happiness. The one thing I did like about being tutored was that it kept my "friend" Tom away as I was always busy with my tutor or studying. I continued to fail my courses however.

A few weeks later I was back in the Seminary Prefect's office and was informed a letter had been sent to my mother about my poor attendance and lousy grades. I was given a final warning "that if I didn't turn things around, I wouldn't be welcome at the seminary anymore." That warning had the opposite effect on me, as it didn't give me incentive to try harder, it gave me a ray of hope I might get out of this place. That's all I thought about after the letter had been sent to my mother. *When was I getting out of this place?*

I began shirking all my school work and just stopped trying all together. One day soon after, I was playing ping pong in the recreation room with another boy when Tom came in with a new friend.

"Give me the paddle," he said with a glare.

"Let us finish our game," I said with a confidence I didn't know I had.

"Give me the paddle, Freddy wets the beddy!"

As he tried to take the paddle from me, a force from within me took over and I shoved him away from me as hard as I could. He backed over a chair and came down hard on his elbow and ran out of the room holding his arm to his chest and cringing in pain crying, "You're gonna get it!"

A few hours later, I was informed Tom had a chipped bone in his elbow and had to be taken to a nearby hospital. I was sitting in the Prefect's office again when I was informed my father was on his way to pick me up.

On the way back to Johnstown, the first thing I did was beg my father to take me back to Ocean City with him.

"Your mother asked me to bring you directly home and that is where we are going, I'm afraid," he said with a strange smile.

I told him how bad that place was.

"I had a feeling that it wasn't for you, Freddy."

I sat there wondering how upset my mother was that I let her down.

"How mad is Mother with me?"

Then he turned my world upside down by saying, "We aren't going back to Johnstown. Freddy, we are all living on 6th Street now…right down from the boardwalk."

My relief, knowing that I wasn't going back to an angry mother cooped up in that tiny apartment to live with my sister and baby brother in Johnstown was too much to measure. I was ecstatic and shouted, "Really?!"

"We're on the way to Ocean City," he said in a way that had a tone of an apology.

Mercersburg Academy in Pennsylvania.

I was nervous about what my mother was going to say to me. I wondered how angry she would be to see me. She was waiting on the porch when we arrived and I was surprised that she rushed to hug me. She didn't mention what happened at the seminary at all and said she was just happy to have me home. I told her for days many stories of how rotten and rough the kids were there and a few weeks later she told me she sent an application for a working scholarship to Mercersburg Academy, one of the most exclusive prep schools on the East Coast. She knew they provided these scholarships to needy families because my brother, Rohn, had already attended and was an excellent student while there.

That summer was spent renting umbrellas and surf mats to tourists just off the hot wooden planks of the boardwalk. It didn't take long to get re-acquainted with Ocean City and with a lot of my friends there. The time passed like a hot summer blur of fun and excitement. In late August, the day came to leave for Mercersburg. Rohn told me so many great things about it, I was actually not nervous about going. "You're just like all the others there...you just have to work the cafeteria a few hours a day," he told me. "You're going to love it."

After the misery I'd endured at the Seminary, I had a feeling this was going to be a much better experience.

Mercersburg was just what you'd expect—a boarding-school with high standards filled with students from wealthier families all over the East Coast. Classes were small, teachers were great and the most important thing was their emphasis on sports. Every student had to be an athlete involved with at least one of the offered sports. I thought about trying out for the football team and the basketball team, but when I stepped into the gym on one cool September morning and smelled the familiar scents of wood and sweat I took a deep long breath and felt alive or re-awakened to something I craved in life. There were guys on wrestling mats doing drills and I couldn't stop myself from joining in.

Outside of wrestling with friends in the sand, I'd no idea about the sport, but when they grouped me with three other boys my age and weight I felt I belonged to something amazing. I don't know if they were taking it easy on me at first or not, but I soon learned if I practiced hard and learned technique I could compete with any one of them.

A good coach there saw that I had some natural ability and spent extra time showing me technique and helping me understand the sport.

"Freddy, you have something that amazes me," the coach said. "Your reflexes are incredible. That's the reason why these wrestlers, who've got a lot more experience than you, are having trouble beating you. It all starts with the takedown in wrestling and you are so quick to respond and counter it's only a matter of time for you…if you stick it out."

This was all the encouragement I needed to hear. I worked for hours on the mat trying to improve my skills. After a few weeks of practice, the coach of the team announced when wrestle-offs would take place. To make the first team and compete for Mercersburg seemed too good to be true, but when the day came to wrestle the other guys in my weight class to make Varsity, I shocked the team and pinned a senior who had been first team the year before, giving the head coach no other option than to have me wrestle first team.

I didn't have the same amount of experience these other athletes had and may not have had the raw talent either, but I did have one thing—motivation to excel. The memory of sitting on the bench powerless while the others played basketball back at that Y.M.C.A. encouraged me to take control on the wrestling mat. I also was motivated by the fact that even though I was serving these more privileged students their meals in the cafeteria, I was on their level as an athlete, especially as a varsity athlete.

Midway through my first season, my brother Rohn came to visit to watch me wrestle a match for the team. He told me how amazed he was I'd made the first string. When it came time for the match I found out I had my hands full against a very good opponent. After two periods I was losing 12-5. And it got worse in the third…with only seconds left on the clock I was losing 15-8 when I somehow mustered the strength to turn and pin the guy right at the buzzer. The joy I felt seeing Rohn up there clapping almost made me cry and I might have, but at that moment my coach grabbed me in his arms and said into my ear, "You are one lucky person. You were givin' me a heart attack out there!"

The working scholarship at Mercersburg was the best thing that could have happened to me. It gave me opportunities to get to know and socialize with not only my classmates, many of whom were privileged and knew it, but I was also making friends with the other students and athletes who were in the same situation I was in as well as the workers there in the kitchen who were mostly African American.

Most of the kitchen staff seemed to be a jolly bunch, but the kitchen manager was a loud, rough guy named Lou, who was pretty harsh with the crew and made no attempt at hiding his racist leanings. He would belittle the kitchen staff all the time and used derogatory language without hesitation. He restrained himself most of the time when ordering the working students like myself around, but it made us angry to hear how he treated them. One of the most popular guys in the kitchen was a young man who was about my age. His name was Judee. He was always smiling and cracking jokes with us. He'd ask us questions about the teams and loved to hear about my wrestling matches. Sometimes, after a shift, he and I and a few of the other servers would sit around playing cards and talking.

"Did you hear what Judee said? Did you hear what Judee did?" were questions I'd hear almost on a daily basis. He just loved making people laugh. One day, as I was walking into the kitchen with a co-worker named Jim, we overheard the kitchen manager laying into the poor guy, calling him a stinkin'- this or a lazy- that and it got both of us steamed.

"I know what we're gonna do."

For every meal there, about twelve of us servers would have to line up behind the swinging kitchen door to have our trays loaded with food to take out and serve. It made a nice orderly presentation that the kitchen manager supervised with great attention for breakfast, lunch and dinner.

"I'll be first in line like usual," my friend said, "And you are usually set there in the back, right?"

"Yes," I agreed.

"Well, today we'll show that guy. And Judee will get the last laugh.

"What do you mean?" I asked.

"When we get out the door, I'm gonna pretend to trip and fall back, if you fall forward with your tray it'll make such a pile of mess ol' Lou will have a conniption."

"I'm in," I said.

It went off just as we hoped; food was flying, silverware was clanging, jaws were dropping and Lou was fuming. My friend Jim took all the blame and was punished with walking the campus patrol for a month straight. The others and I claimed innocence. "We couldn't help but fall over Jim," I said. Later that night we sat around laughing as Judee described the look on Lou's face when it happened. It was priceless.

"Was it worth it?" I asked Jim.

"I'd do it again in a heart beat," he said as he laughed with Judee.

Hearing how that kitchen manager talked to his staff was really my first encounter with racism, but I didn't really fully understand what it was until the night Jim, Judee, and I left campus to see a movie in the small town there. We were all sitting there in the half-full theatre in the dark waiting for the movie to start, when an usher came over to our little group and said, "Your place is upstairs!"

We were all astonished.

"Why can't he sit with us? We're all together," I said to the man.

"In this theatre, all colored people sit upstairs."

We all got up and walked out of the theatre together. Jim immediately started talking about what we could do to get even with that guy, but I looked at Judee's face and just said, "Let it go, Jim."

Five minutes later we were all walking back toward campus laughing and cutting up about something new.

After three years I'd made a lot of friends, joined various clubs and was even named Captain of the Letterman's Club, but still struggled with classes and was just barely getting by academically.

On the first day of my senior year, I was called to the headmaster's office and he lowered the boom, "Freddy, I have some bad news for you. Your grades are not good enough for you to remain at this academy."

I was stunned. I was one of the best wrestlers on the team. I was elected Captain by my teammates. I was the President of the Varsity Club, and I quickly reminded him of this.

"I'm sorry, Freddy," he said solemnly.

Ninety-nine percent of the students there would have just walked out of the office at that point but I defiantly stayed and made the case that I was important to the school for reasons more important than academics. I was important for the moral of the school. After minutes of trying to convince this man of my importance and desperately trying to persuade him I'd do what ever it took to get my grades up and succeed, he broke down and said he'd give me one last chance.

I hid my smile until I got out the door of his office, but once I was out I was exhilarated not only by the fact I'd dodged a bullet and was going to be able to stay on campus and graduate, but I'd also felt a power of being able to completely change someone's mind with words.

My final season on the mat was my best and at the end I participated in the National Prep School Championship tournament. I muscled through four tough matches to make the finals. It was a pretty big deal to even participate in this event, but nobody from my family had the time or money to come out to watch. As I sat on the side of the mat there waiting for my turn, the memory of Rohn looking down from the stands while I waited to get a chance in the basketball game five years earlier came back to me. I sat there and looked up in the stands that were full of spectators and I couldn't believe my eyes. My father was there intently watching another match that was going on. I could not believe it. He hadn't told me he was coming. It was a complete shock.

When I went out to wrestle, I was filled with motivation and pride. I had a chance to go out on top, and my father was there to see it. I gave it everything I had—for Mercersburg, for my team mates, for that rotten basketball coach back at the Y, for my old ping pong "buddy" Tom, for my Mother and for my Father, but my opponent was better. I lost 10-5 and took the silver medal. As I walked off the mat, I looked at my coach and teammates and shrugged…then looked up into the crowd to find my father…he wasn't there anymore. I thought for sure he'd stop by to talk with me afterward, but he never did. On the team bus riding back to campus I was left to wonder, *Was he ever really there?*

A few months later, thanks to some helpful teachers and a lot of luck, I graduated and went back to Ocean City full of great memories and something I'd never felt before, a sense of pride.

4

1954-1960
Black and White

After graduating from Mercersburg, I spent the summer working at the beach in Ocean City. My friends and I spent a lot of time carousing and seemed to be on a mission to drink the town dry of its entire supply of beer. The town never seemed to run out of beer, but I ran out of time. By September, even though I'd received athletic scholarship offers from several universities, a couple of my friends and I decided to get the two years of required service in the armed forces over with. At the time, it was a mandatory duty, and we thought why not get it over with?

For the next two years, my life was filled with repetitious and tedious drills and assignments at military bases in Georgia and South Carolina. While I understood the rationale for the country to have an Army ready in case of a threat of war, I have always felt guilty that so many served and suffered in real wars, and all I had to do was play pretend war at these bases stateside.

After two long boring years in the service, where the only fun I had was away from base on leave, I decided to apply for a scholarship t the University of Maryland. I met with the wrestling coach and was soon set up with a meal plan and a dorm room with other wrestlers at College Park. Because of my love of sports, I knew from day one I wanted to major in physical education.

While I struggled in classes just as I did in high school, I found subjects I began to take an interest in. One of the instructors read a quote from Plato one day that always stayed with me, "A child is at their learning best while at play."

The first year went fairly well, but I didn't have the competitive edge I had at Mercersburg, and there was another big problem. My older brother Lynn was a talented, self-taught pianist and convinced me to join his band playing an upright bass. I had a natural ear for music and had picked on bass before, but I had a lot to learn. In about two weeks, he had me ready to play gigs with a drummer and saxophone player.

Trying to mix the lifestyle of a musician and college wrestler was like trying to make ice without a freezer. It just didn't work, and during my second year I quit the team. Since you were given a room and meals at the University, I felt more like I was owned and the sport began to feel like a job as opposed to being fun.

During the spring of that year, a friend introduced me to the sport of golf and I was hooked after a couple of games. The university had an indoor driving range where he and I would spend all of our spare time hitting golf balls. After a while, I became pretty good and played on the university course as often as I could.

Another thing happened that spring that would change my life forever. I'd been dating a girl from Baltimore for a few months at the time, but on one of the trips into Ocean City to play a gig with my brother, an old friend came up to me and said, "I've got the perfect match for you. She goes to school with me at Salisbury State and you've got to meet her!"

"But I already have a girlfriend," I told her.

"I understand…but you just have to meet her."

I agreed to meet her and my friend set it up for the next night in town. Her name was Michaele Anne – yes, Michaele – her friends called her Mike. We met at my friend's house and when I walked into her place and saw her from across the room, all I could see were her beautiful brown eyes. To say that we hit it off would be an understatement. She was a high school athlete and stand-out on her basketball team. She even set a school record for scoring 51 points in a game. Talk about a perfect match. That night we talked for hours and I just couldn't seem to hear enough about her.

Fred met his wife Michaele on a blind date.

I never saw the girl from Baltimore again after that date. Mike was a waitress at a nearby restaurant. We dated throughout the summer and that fall we were married. The following summer, Kathi, the first of our seven children was born. I was a father now and working and doing everything and anything to make money—playing gigs with our band, "The Red Notes," a couple of times a week, running a cash register at a liquor store by night and renting umbrellas and surf mats on the boardwalk by day. I was busy, but we were living in a trailer park and just getting by. A year later, our second child, David, was born and I knew I had to get back to school to finish my degree. At Maryland I'd been pursuing a Physical Education degree, so naturally I wanted to finish, but there was no way that we could afford to travel back and forth to College Park a good two hours away. Fortunately, there was a branch campus about thirty minutes from the shore, so I looked into enrolling there.

"You can't go to Maryland State!" a friend laughed at me.

"Why not?" I knew that it was an all black college, but I was more interested in the fact they offered a physical education degree and since it was part of the University of Maryland they would accept the credits I'd already earned there. Growing up in the area, I knew of the racial divide. It was an attitude that prevailed in the area for years. After all, when I was in elementary school in town, I remember the black children were bused to a school about fifteen miles away.

Imbedded in my mind was a memory of an incident that happened when I was younger and selling papers on the boardwalk. The "rule" was there were no "colored people" allowed on the beach. Bold as it could be, on the end of every street that entered the beach, a sign was posted, "NO COLORED ALLOWED."

I watched one day from the boardwalk as a black woman dressed in all white walked onto the sand with some white children. She was probably tasked to baby-sit them there on the beach. There she was walking in the sand, when I saw police rushing in her direction as if she were on fire or something. Apparently, so many people had already complained there was a "colored lady" on the beach the men treated her as if she were an escaped prisoner and forced her and the children to get off the beach. As a child, I couldn't get over how hostile the men were over the fact she was just not their color.

"You'll be the only white guy there," my friend laughed.

I asked Mike if she had any problems with me going there. She said absolutely not, but her father would probably have some words for me.

In the early 1960s, the Eastern Shore of Maryland was loaded with cultural strife. The small town of Cambridge was becoming a national hot bed for the Civil Rights movement. Riots and protests for equal access to public areas like beaches and integration in public schools were starting to heat up. Even though I'd read and heard about violent protests taking place, it didn't sway me from my goal of getting my degree.

For whatever reason, the prospect of being the only white guy on campus didn't faze me. Sure, there were a lot of ignorant and racist people—I just didn't talk with anyone about the subject. For me, it was a way of getting my education and degree so I could do better and my family could, too.

I remember the queasiness I felt the first day as I pulled my car into the parking lot on campus. I looked around and saw nothing but black students and instructors walking this way and that. I remember thinking, *this is how they feel when they go into a store that is full of white people.*

It was daunting, but I got out of the car and headed for the registrar's office. When I got there, it was filled with students in line and faculty helping them with their schedules. As I stood in line I got a lot of curious looks. Then the guy who was in front of me turned around and quietly said, "This is the line to register for school."

"I know. I'm registering today."

You could hear a pin drop as all eyes fell on me for a moment. Then, from out of the blue, I was approached by another student there and he stated with a big grin, "Welcome to Maryland State…home of the hawks!"

All the tension evaporated from the room after that and I began to feel at ease. When I started classes, I was a bit worried about the backlash I might receive from some of the other students. It turned out I was the only white student there my first year. It was hard not to feel somewhat intimidated but I heard and saw nothing negative at all from anyone on campus.

Classes went well and I quickly became friends with the other students who were studying physical education. When I found out there was a golf team, one of the first things I did was inquire about playing for the school. Back at College Park I thought I was pretty good and really had the itch to play again. Playing for the school seemed like fun and a way to play for free.

Breaking the Color Barrier at Maryland State College.

I'll never forget our coach, Mr. Briggs. He wasn't much at teaching golf, but he always went out of his way to make sure we had a place to practice.

"For real?" he asked, the day I inquired about trying out for the team. He watched me hit some balls off a tee and scratched his head and said, "Country clubber?"

"No, just love playing," I said

"For real? Well, I know we could use you."

On that day, I met a guy who would soon become one of the best friends I ever had. Bob Taylor was 6 feet and 4 inches tall and 240 pounds of muscle. He was the best player on the golf team and also a star player on the football team. For whatever reason, we were paired up to practice together and through mutual appreciation of skills we became fast friends. Two guys could not have been more different, but we saw eye to eye on the golf course.

"You're good, but Fred, you lazy….you gotta follow through on all your swings."

"You have no idea how lazy this guy can be," I said with a laugh.

I knew exactly what he meant. I also knew he was right and thanked him. I think the fact I could take criticism so easily impressed Bob, too. Midway through that first season he and I decided to practice at a nearby course called Winter Quarters. As we walked the course, we reached an area where Bob hit a shot into a sand trap. He hit his ball out—we putted and moved on to the next hole.

As we walked on, a man approached us and said, "Boy, let me tell you something! On this golf course, we rake the bunker after hitting out of it. You git that?!"

First of all, to call an African American "boy" was a clear way to degrade him, but Bob also knew we'd both neglected to rake the bunkers on that day and he was being profiled. By the look on his face, at first I thought he was going to explode with rage, but he immediately calmed down and said, "Yes, sir."

We both walked back to the bunker together and I could hear the man grumble and spit.

"Now you know what it feels like to be a black man around here," Bob stated.

As we got near to the sand trap I reached down and grabbed the rake and started smoothing the sand over and said, "Well then, this'll piss 'em off."

I knew Bob was a great guy, but we became better friends from that day forward. I also knew that no matter what else happened on or off campus, I had his back and he had mine.

The golf team would travel to various black colleges on the East Coast and along the way we'd stop for gas and food. The looks and sometimes comments we'd get as five black guys and one white would get out of a car together were anything from comical to downright frightening. And these were reactions from both white people and black. As a team, we never avoided talking about the elephant in the room and most of the time made a big joke of it. I loved to tell the story of how one night Mike and I had gone out to dinner and left the kids with a sitter back at the trailer park we lived in. When we returned, the young woman who was watching the kids told us how she was terrified and worried for me because a large, scary, black man had come by asking where I was. She said, with a very worried tone, "He said he probably knew where to find you." We all had a great laugh at that one.

On one occasion, as we pulled onto the campus at Morgan State College in Baltimore, I noticed a guy named Big Daddy Lipscomb sitting in the parking lot with a bunch of other guys as we got out. He wasn't called Big Daddy for nothing. He stood about 6-foot and 7-inches and weighed well over 300 pounds. As we got out of the car I saw his eyes light up as if he was seeing a ghost.

"Who the hell is that little honkey ridin' with you all?" he asked with some intensity in his voice as he glared at me.

I think it is safe to say that I was more than nervous at that point, but Bob went right over to him and said a few words that turned Big Daddy's glare into a smile. I don't know what Bob said, and I was a little too distracted to ask, but it did the trick and we went on to win the match that afternoon. That year we also celebrated the fact we won the Conference and did we ever celebrate! Overall, joining that team and making friends like these was one of the best things I ever did.

Bob was a great golfer, but he was a better football player. After college he was drafted by the New York Giants. A few months after graduation, I received a letter from him telling me how much fun he had playing golf, but more importantly, how much he enjoyed our friendship. He also explained it was the first experience being friends with someone of another race. He said growing up in the South, he was never allowed or able to get close to any white person. I still have the letter to this day.

During the three years it took me to graduate, I took some playful ribbing from some of my friends, and also heard some mean-spirited words from both white and black people who saw me coming and going to and from campus.

One hot afternoon, after eighteen holes with Bob, we pulled into a gas station near campus that made some of the best fried chicken in the world. We were laughing hard about something as I got out of the car and I told Bob I would go in and buy a couple of cold drinks. When I went inside the place, the smell of the fried chicken was overwhelming. I walked up to the counter and ordered two chicken dinners to surprise Bob.

"What're you doin'?" the man asked.

"What?" I asked with a confused smile on my face.

"I said, what do you think you doin'?"

"Buying some chicken," I said.

"Boss says you ain't buyin' it here."

I looked over in the corner where a big man in a white apron was looking me in the eyes and turning his head back and forth with contempt. I'd bought the chicken many times before and the same man happily served me. It didn't take me long to add it up, so I walked out disgusted. I never mentioned it to Bob.

Later that night, Bob and I were playing pool at a nearby bar. It was a bar I would only feel comfortable going to with Bob. Meaning—I was the only white guy in the place. We were in a room just off the bar that was hardly big enough for a pool table, but we were laughing and drinking beer and talking with some young women who walked in to watch us play.

After a game, Bob walked off to use the bathroom and as soon as he left the room, three men walked in.

"You best get!" one of the guys said to me with a scary and harsh stare as he forced the pool stick from my hand.

The three of them walked me to the door and I walked out and sat in the car. A minute later Bob walked to the car as I sat there in the dark.

"Hey, man, those guys were just funnin' with you," he said.

"I don't think so, Bob."

"Come on man, they were just foolin'"

"No, I'd better be getting home anyway."

By graduation day I was the father of one daughter and two sons–with a third son on the way. It felt like the weight of the world was on my shoulders, but I had finally earned a college degree and was sure I'd get a good job in the near future.

My time, at what is now called the University of Maryland Eastern Shore, was a great learning experience and it gave me and my family the opportunity for a better life. I'll never forget the kindness and encouragement I received from my professors and classmates while I was there.

At the graduation ceremony my wife Mike attended with my children in tow and smiled down at me when I crossed the stage to receive my diploma. I wasn't sure what our future was going to be, but I knew, that day for sure, we could make it through anything.

5

1963-1968
Rag-Tag to Viking Football

After graduation I was offered a job teaching physical education at a nearby Catholic school in Salisbury, Maryland called St. Francis. To say I quickly became bored teaching kids how to do proper jumping jacks and officiating kickball games would be an understatement.

Back at Mercersburg I'd tried out and made the football team, but the coach never let me in a game for fear that I'd be injured and ruin my wrestling season. I'd spent lots of time on the sidelines watching and learning the game from a coach's point of view and even dreaming of being a coach myself one day.

After a month of teaching, I got the idea to start a football program at the school with the middle school-aged kids. I asked and the school administrators thought it was a crazy idea, but said, "Why not?"

It wasn't easy. I had to find eleven kids who would even sign up for the team. I pled with uninterested, non-athletic kids just to fill out the roster, but I eventually did it. We had no uniforms, so I went to the local Salvation Army that had a youth sports program and asked if we could borrow some. Sure enough, they let us have their old, smelly uniforms and equipment.

A week later, I had the kids on the field drawing up plays in the dirt. I was delusionally positive about the whole idea. I was simply preaching football ideas and concepts I'd picked up on the sidelines at Mercersburg, or watching the University of Maryland Terrapins play. A lot of the kids wanted to quit that first week, but I promised them an "A" in gym class if they stuck with it.

After a few weeks of practice, I even went so far as to call an area coach at a nearby middle school and challenged him to a scrimmage game. He told me he'd never even heard of our school, but I promised we would be a formidable opponent and he agreed to play us.

Everyone at the school was excited about the idea. Even the girls formed a cheerleading team and made their own uniforms. They even gave the team a nickname, "The Frankies."

The date was set and I was off to conquer the world with a rag-tag bunch of kids who hardly knew how to play the game. I spent almost every waking hour thinking of ways to prepare and motivate these kids. We had several practices and some of the kids were actually pretty quick to pick up on the things I tried to teach them about playing.

To get an idea of what I was in for, a week before our game, I went to watch another middle school game being played nearby. Watching the formations and plays these teams were using made me feel comfortable. They were familiar and seemed to be very similar to what I'd been teaching my guys. Sitting in the stands, however, gave me a different perspective on things. I could not believe the things being shouted by the parents in the stands. One father stood and hollered and harassed his son about his performance after almost every play. I felt bad for the kid and felt for the first time the pressure some of these kids were under to meet the crazy standards their parents had set for them. I walked over to the guy and said, "Do really think yelling at your son like that is helping?"

"He's not my son," the man stated.

"He's not your son?" I asked, a little bewildered.

"He ain't my son playing like that!" he shouted loud enough for most of the people in the stands to hear and then stomped down the steps and drove off.

I could hardly believe it…that someone could take a game that's supposed to be for fun and turn it into something so ugly. I always remembered that guy when I felt I might be taking things too seriously with my players. I also had a short meeting with their parents soon after and described the behavior I'd seen and told them all I'd have none of it.

"If you want to play a sport, go ahead and play it on your own," I said. "Otherwise, let's just let the kids have fun trying to win!"

On the day of the big game I was surprised to see one of the priests from our school in attendance. He was apparently a football fan or very curious as to how we'd do against a real opponent. I was in seventh heaven—living a dream of coaching my own football team and to me, it was as big as the Super Bowl.

When we got to the field, I looked across the grass at the other team with their bright red uniforms and shiny helmets and for the first time, felt intimidated. They were made up of about fifty kids who all seemed a lot larger than my players…we were twelve altogether dressed in grass-stained white jerseys, dented helmets and mismatched equipment. I wanted to herd my guys back on to the bus and head home immediately to save us all from the embarrassment, but for some reason we stayed. I was fearful we would be carrying half my team to the hospital before halftime and I would be sued for all I was worth for pretending to know what I was doing.

The game began and the one thing we had going for us was that we had an amazing athlete – one of the fastest 13 year olds you can imagine – playing quarterback. Every play we drew up in the sand was tossed for quarterback sneaks and quarterback sweep plays that had him tearing down the sidelines for dear life. By the time we reached the fourth quarter he'd rushed for three touchdowns against our opponents' two.

The game ended, and "The Frankies" held on to win by seven. I felt like I was the next Vince Lombardi and destined for the Hall of Fame.

The priest from school, whose name was Father Fink, came over to me after the game and congratulated me for winning. He was so proud our school won and praised me for being able to turn this bunch of kids into a respectable team. It was hard to get another scrimmage after that game, but the thrill of actually coaching a football game and winning got me through the rest of the year of teaching.

At the end of the school year, I went back to my various jobs at the beach and the Red Notes band I was in with my brother was popular enough to actually make money. Mike and I were the parents of five children now and I was literally working day and night seven days a week to keep ahead.

One day in early August, I got a phone call from the head of St. Elizabeth's High School in Wilmington, Delaware. It was a priest on the other end named Father Burns who said, "How would you like to be the head football coach here at St. Elizabeth's?"

I almost passed out. After gathering myself, I said, "Well, it sounds like a good opportunity." Why in the world would the head of a Catholic high school contact me and offer me a job to coach their team? I never coached a legitimate team before. I thought he had me mixed up with some other coach or something and called the wrong person. Then he told me I was recommended by Father Fink from St. Francis, the guy who attended the one and only game I ever coached. They apparently were good friends and he was willing to gamble on an inexperienced newcomer to the field of coaching.

I sent him a glowing self-promotional resume letter that would make someone think I was ready to be an NFL coach, yet all the while worried someone was going to catch on I wasn't really a qualified football coach. I'd never even played a down of football in high school or college. Being on the sidelines all season long at Mercersburg surely didn't qualify me as an expert or even ready to coach high school football.

When I went for my interview, I nervously waited outside of Father Burns' office expecting him to come out and apologize for making a clerical error and calling the wrong guy in for the job. Instead, after about thirty seconds, he came into the room and said, "You've got the job....practice starts in two weeks."

I gulped at the prospect and immediately thought of how unprepared I was, but I quickly said, "I'll be ready."

As I sat there, I looked into his eyes and wondered what he saw in me, and then he said something that I'll never forget, "Fred, if you never want to make a mistake, never risk anything."

Our fifth child, Darin, was born only a couple months before, but within a week of the interview, Mike and I found a place for the seven of us not too far from the school. I'll never be able to express how grateful I was when she so confidently said that she'd move anywhere we needed to live to make things work.

Soon, I began to feel excited about the new life that lay ahead. My friends were surprised and a little bewildered to hear I'd landed a real coaching job. My father, on the other hand, was a little less enthusiastic about it, to say the least. He'd been back home for a few years at this point. And by home, I mean about the twelfth apartment they'd lived in since moving to Ocean City so many years before.

"What do you know about the sport? How can you coach something you didn't even play?" he asked pessimistically. He had played in both high school and college, but instead of offering any real advice, he just said, "You're gonna be sorry."

Those words stung at first, but they turned out to be the motivation that fueled me to succeed. I spent hours learning the formations and plays that were used and my will to succeed was beyond measure. *If I could only pass this on to the players, we couldn't lose*, I thought.

I arrived in Wilmington ready for action my first day there and met with the other coaches. A long-time coach retired the year before and his defensive coach assumed he'd be taking over the team that year, but fortunately that didn't happen. He was a good coach and very good with the players. I worried at some point he'd show anger towards me for getting the job he'd wanted, but he was a good man and never seemed to hold it against me and never brought up my lack of experience.

I'll never forget the first day of practice looking out at about 60 high school kids as I chomped at the bit, ready for the challenge. I couldn't believe the talent and swagger of the team I'd inherited. It turned out this bunch was happy to have a new coach and pushed me as much as I pushed them on that first day of drills.

This was a pretty big deal in Wilmington, Delaware. Coaching at this level brought with it lots of expectations from the school and the local community. It didn't faze me at all though. I had a kid playing quarterback who had been a huge factor on offense the year before, and I don't know if my confidence rubbed off on them or their confidence rubbed off on me, but that first year, I felt pretty good before the season started.

The St. Elizabeth High School Football Team. Fred is front row left.

After a few weeks of practice in the hot August sun that streamed through the tall buildings of downtown, we were ready.

The first game of the season was a real test against one of the stronger programs in the area. It rained like cats and dogs throughout the game and as the fourth quarter began, the score was tied. I'd never even been close to a situation like this before and the pressure was overwhelming, but I stayed composed and told the players on our last drive of the game they were "the best team I'd ever coached, but we still had work to do." On fourth and long inside our opponent's thirty yard line, I called a quarterback sneak up the middle and it went for ten yards. In all the rain and mud, I was just trying to protect the football, but it worked. So I called it again, and it worked again. Inside the ten yard line with under a minute to play, I called it for a third time and we scored to win the game. My players were so happy they carried me off the field as if we'd won the Super Bowl.

Talk about going from the outhouse to the big house. I was on cloud nine floating for a week. And it didn't stop there. The team was a scrappy bunch with a lot of swagger, they loved their new coach…and we were winning. We actually won our first eight games in a row and the newspapers were calling me for interviews. I soon began getting cocky and even letting some of the players come up with their own plays for fun. They came up with all kinds of crazy stuff and I'd say, "Why not?"

They loved it. It was loose and prioritized fun, which apparently was the polar opposite approach as to how the coach treated them the year before. The team responded with an incredible will to win games and before long we were preparing for the Conference Title game.

A week before the game, I found the principal of the school in my office with some very bad news. He told me that five of our best players were caught drinking at a party over the weekend. I was shattered, knowing I would have to suspend them even though it would mean we'd probably lose the big game the following week. The principal said, "Well, it is your decision, Coach."

In a way, he was telling me he'd be okay if I didn't punish the kids but I knew I had to. I was visited by parents and faculty trying to convince me these players should play despite news of their drinking making its way around campus. I did the right thing—held them out of the game, and we lost our chance of winning the Conference Title by a touchdown. Without our quarterback, star receiver and best defensive player, we still played a great game. It was a tough loss, but it was a moral victory for the school and the local fans of the team had something to cheer about—they had a successful team.

After that first year with such a talented team, I thought coaching football was easy as cake, but was I ever wrong. The next year, despite my confidence, we could hardly win a game. Gone were the cocky rowdy kids who made up a lot of the team the year before. Now, the team was full of kids who actually needed intensive coaching to perform. I was in trouble and the pressure to win was awful. After a couple losses, I got visits from faculty members and the school booster club asking what was wrong, and heard taunts from the parents in the stands during games.

During that second year I witnessed one of the most horrific things I've ever seen in sports. The opposing team's quarterback lay on the field after being sacked by one of our players. His coach picked him up off the grass and asked him what was wrong. The player's arm just dangled from his shoulder as he told the coach he couldn't throw the football any more. I heard the coach say to him, "I know what you did, you separated your shoulder…I know what to do!" I watched as the coached pulled at the kid's arm and tried to pry the arm back into his shoulder socket as the kid winced and cried in pain. It didn't work and the poor kid eventually fell to the ground and passed out. Ambulances were called and he was soon taken off to the hospital. I can still feel my skin crawl the same way it did that day when I found out that the kid never had a separated shoulder.

The coach was trying to fix an arm broken much lower than the shoulder by trying to force it into place.

Maybe if I'd had the chance to coach another year or two, I might have turned it around, but after five games, the school administration was talking about replacing me. Mike and I were stressing out at the time as she was pregnant with our sixth child. I probably shouldn't have told her of the stress I was under, but it was hard to contain.

"Everything is going to work out. Whatever happens, we will get by," she told me.

She also showed me her unbelievable abilities to manage the house, kids and even taking on any work she could manage to help out.

Fortunately, around this time, I was offered a job as a Director of Sports just down the street at the Catholic Youth Organization of Delaware. It paid more than coaching, without all the pressure to win every game. And I wouldn't have to deal with the parents who thought their kid was destined to be the next Heisman Trophy winner and I just wasn't playing him enough.

With our sixth child on the way and having just bought our first house, the decision was an easy one to make, but I didn't know at the time that it would have such a profound impact on my life.

6

1968-1973
Wilmington

The Catholic Youth Organization, also referred to as CYO, had many youth sports programs and leagues in and around the Wilmington area. My job as youth sports director was to make sure things ran smoothly—refs got to games on time, teams had coaches, and facilities were maintained. It was crazy at first, but things became more orderly as time went on.

Working there for a few years, I got to watch my children play and grow as they participated in some of the sports programs in the area. But sadly, I was also in the position to see and hear about the many problems within the system.

Working at the CYO gave a whole new meaning and insight into the world of organized sports for kids. Since it was a religious organization I figured the people from the bottom to the top would look at sports as a great opportunity to develop character. What I found, however, was that we were teaching kids to be characters – and not good ones. Sure, overall, parents were respectful and caring for their kids, but the surprising thing was the amount of ugly behavior I would see or hear about through phone calls from coaches or parents.

Perhaps the worst incident, and one that drove me to begin to say that something is seriously wrong with sports for children, was the football fiasco.

I was at home eating dinner when I got a call from a frantic parent. "So what are you going to do about what happened at our football game today?"

"What happened?" I asked.

According to the caller, after the game was over and the winning team was getting on the bus for their ride home, the opposing team's players began to pick up rocks and throw them at the winners. Several players were injured. One player happened to be sitting next to the window was seriously injured. As a rock made impact with the window shattered glass hit him in the face. He was rushed to the hospital and required stitches on his face and neck.

As the director of the CYO it was my job to penalize any team or player(s) who violated the rules. In this incident I decided to suspend the whole team for the season. It seemed to me that after that violent incident, the punishment would be accepted by everyone, but that wasn't the case. The punished team's parents protested all the way up the chain of command and because the clergy were closely involved with what went on in the program, I was told I would have to rescind the punishment. According to my superiors, "It was the act of only a few players, so how could you punish the whole team?"

I disagreed and held the whole team accountable, even the players who watched and did nothing to stop what was going on.

I was very upset the people positioned at the highest levels of this religious community would not only get involved in the decision, but they would not back me up on something so violent and wrong.

The ugliness I began to see on almost on a daily basis began to turn my faith in these people from disappointment to anger. I began to realize there were a lot of bad people out there working with youngsters as volunteer coaches. There were so many complaints that first year, I put a suggestion box outside my office in hope people would let off steam writing on a card instead of getting in my face.

Most of the cards contained complaints about officiating and poor coaching and stories of how their son or daughter wasn't getting enough playing time, but I was also getting stories of just how verbally abusive coaches and parents were being while attending the games. I got so disgusted by the things I was reading I almost took the box down one day. I was tired of hearing the complaints, but then I read a card from a young boy who simply wrote: MY COACH WON'T LEAVE ME ALONE. CAN I PLEASE PLAY ON ANOTHER TEAM? He even put his name on the piece of paper.

I looked through the rosters of the teams and found his name, as well as the coaches of his team. After contacting the parents, I was surprised they just brushed it off as their kid's imagination. *It was probably the reason the boy dropped the note in the box himself*, I thought.

I had a hunch it wasn't his imagination so I decided to look into the story and soon heard from reliable sources there was a coach, a local priest, who had a reputation for getting a little too close to his players. I privately talked with a young man who knew the coach personally.

"He's a bad man," he said.

"What do you mean by bad?"

"He gets too close to the kids!"

"He'll give them things, a lot of things, but he wants something back."

I knew what he meant by that, and it disgusted me.

"How do you know this stuff?" I asked.

"He was my coach three years ago. I quit the team and haven't played since."

That was an ugly can of worms, which at that at the time, I didn't know how to handle properly. I talked with a co-worker about taking the story to my superiors, but I was told to "let it drop." Working under the banner of the Catholic Church, I always had the "they are never wrong" impression, not to mention if I were to suggest one of their own was in any way "unholy" I might lose my job.

So I didn't rush downtown to the police station and file a complaint, but I did tell a police officer he should keep an eye on the guy. I told him I had my suspicions.

For the kid who'd dropped the note in the box, I made a roster switch that placed him immediately on another team and I hoped things would be different for him there.

This incident made me think of something I had never thought of before. *How many more sick people were out there who use sports as an open door to reach kids at their most vulnerable?* While I was concerned about parents and coaches, here was another reason for the need for training, but also programs to protect kids.

At this time, four of our children were involved in youth sports programs in the area and Mike and I had our hands full getting them here and there for practices and games.

My son John was the baseball player in the family. He had a great coach whom I witnessed teaching discipline, respect and how to play the game with honor. I used to marvel and love how well this coach was teaching my son the important life skills that all kids need to develop to succeed in life.

The coach had an assistant who seemed like an alright guy. One day as I was picking John up from practice, his car pulled up and John was inside. I thought nothing of it at the moment, but as we were driving home I noticed that John had a brand new top-of- the-line catcher's mitt.

"Where did you get that glove?" I asked.

"Coach Al gave it to me," he said.

"Where had you been when I picked you up at practice?"

"Coach Al took me to the store and got me a drink."

"Give me that glove. John, you are not allowed to accept anything like that from any coach without talking to me about it first. And you are not allowed ever to get in any coach's car without talking to me first either."

Anger built up in me and I couldn't wait until I got in the house to call the assistant coach. When I did, I told him to stay away from my son and I will be talking to the head coach about this.

The coach quit after that day and never showed up again. Two years later a story about him appeared in the local paper for his arrest for pedophilia.

One day, my oldest daughter, Kathi, came home from softball practice to tell me a story of how her coach was actually encouraging some of the players on her team to shoplift things for him.

"Where did you get this idea?" I asked.

"He told some of the girls to bring candy to the next game and they said they didn't have any money…so he told them to just steal some."

I asked her to tell me if he ever mentioned anything like that again. I went to her next game and re-introduced myself to the guy to make sure he realized I was the director of the CYO. He denied he told anyone to steal, but after our confrontation he quit coaching the team.

Another time, my son Eric came home from his Little League game and talked about how hot it was at the game and how hard it was to play in the heat.

"I don't want to play baseball again Dad," he said.

I said, "Why not"?

He replied, "When we got to the game today, the coach said nobody gets a drink of water until we score a run."

I couldn't believe a sane adult would do such a thing. I looked at the thermometer hanging outside and it was a balmy 93 degrees.

The saddest part was, that because of this coach, Eric never had the motivation to play baseball again.

I couldn't believe some of the stories I heard from my own children, not to mention the stories of physical and sexual abuse I'd heard in private conversations with parents of other kids within the CYO organization.

When my son John asked to join a soccer league, he asked if I'd be the team's coach. I'd played a little bit of soccer as a youngster, but I knew I needed a lot of help relearning the rules, skills, and in general, the strategies of the game. This wasn't a

CYO affiliated league and I'd never signed up to be a coach like this before.

When I went to ask questions about how things were structured, the director handed me a list of children's names with their phone numbers and the name of the field we could use for practice.

"Start practice. Season starts in two weeks. Good luck!" he barked.

"Are there any instructional programs for people like me who need a refresher course on coaching soccer?" I asked.

"We don't have the time for that. Ask around. Other coaches will help you. Good luck!"

I did ask around and got help from some of the other coaches, but it wasn't enough. In two weeks, I'd managed to get the kids together three times for practice before the season started. Fortunately, some of the kids knew the sport better than I did, and really helped make up for my lack of experience when we talked about how we were going to score and defend.

As we played our first game I noticed that familiar sound again—a parent, who from the time the clock started to the end of the game, shouted out to her son things like, "Hustle, hustle, hustle!...Come on!...You can do better than that!"

She was trying to totally control her son from the sidelines and I could see on his face how embarrassed he was by it.

I walked over to her and said, "Listen, your son is one of the best players on the field and I appreciate your encouragement, but if you can't lay off him, you are going to have to go home. I really don't like to see such hate in a little kid's eyes."

She was dumbfounded. She'd apparently never heard anything like it before. She looked at me for a second with a strange tight-mouthed grin on her face and then just fumed off.

Throughout that season, I had to remind her to tone it down from time to time, but she actually got better and near the end she wasn't yelling any more at all.

There were a few other things I witnessed that year that left a powerful impression. I watched an opposing coach chew out his son in front of his teammates and to emphasize his point, hurled a soccer ball at his face. Another time I watched a parent, after a game, physically pick up his young boy and toss him, literally toss him, into the back of a van. There were many parents there to witness this abuse, but nobody did a thing. It sickened me to watch.

Why wasn't anyone doing anything about this? I wondered. Why were people allowed to coach and run programs without any real training in how to deal with children properly?

I brought it up with my superiors and only got blank looks and excuses that it was all too much to handle.

That is when I decided to create the first ever coach's certification program in America for coaches in the CYO and told coaches if they wanted to participate, they would have to go through an educational program that would teach them to prioritize the child's positive experience over teaching them how important it was to win.

Some of the coaches were threatened by this approach. Some even tried to get me fired for wasting their time, but I stuck to my guns throughout. I made a rule that only teams with coaches who were certified through the training could advance to the playoffs in any sport – and that got their attention.

I remember one of the coaches complaining, "This is bullshit. I'm not coaching under these terms!"

"Sorry to see you go!" I told him knowing that letting him go was the best thing I could do for his players.

At first they viewed me as a pariah, but by the next season for most of the sports that were offered through the organization, almost one hundred percent had gone through a certification program that made them better coaches and improved the whole experience for the kids.

The irony of sports for children is that what can be such a great learning experience, can be turned around by people who could care less about kids...people who are more interested in claiming a victory for themselves as coaches, or as gloating parents who see themselves making kids into star athletes.

"Why do I have to come to this thing, I've been coaching for ten years?" was the typical comment received. I would try to satisfy these people by telling them what a great job they were doing as a coach and I hoped they would share their knowledge with some of the newcomers.

Basically, at the certification events, I would present the coaches with concepts and questions to think about, such as, "What role does winning have in kids' sports? Or, "Why do you think kids come out for sports in the first place?"

After one of the sessions, a coach came up to me and said, to my astonishment, "Do you think I ought to be a coach?"

I was stunned. I figured he was coming up to tell me he thought I was wasting his time and he wanted to leave. As I sat there in bewilderment, I said to him "Why do you ask me that question?"

He said, "In that last discussion we had about the role of winning, I heard many of these guys talk about people like me who just come out and do everything to win games and championships. That's all I've ever done in the past eight years of coaching and I never thought of these things before. It's always been win, win, win. Never anything about how kids feel. I feel a lot of guilt for the way I've treated some of the kids through the years."

I said to him, "Coach, you have just told me something that will last for me for a lifetime. You have just told me the value of having a training program for coachesand no one should ever be allowed to coach kids until they go through a program like this."

As I watched him walk away, I pictured millions of children's coaches saying that to themselves in the future. I was on a mission and nothing would stop me now.

Most people don't like change, however. When the local newspaper in Wilmington wrote a front page story about my mandatory certification programs for all coaches, I received many hateful and threatening phone calls.

Even though you believe you are right in what you are doing, there is always an element of doubt that says to you, "Maybe they're right. Maybe I am trying to do too much, too fast."

Then one day, I read an article in *Newsday* magazine that was sent to me by one of the coaches I'd had in a clinic. It was written by Robin Roberts, the Hall of Fame baseball pitcher from the Philadelphia Phillies. The title of the article was "STRIKE OUT LITTLE LEAGUE!" In the article, Robin Roberts described everything I believed and had seen throughout my early career in youth sports. He said, point blank, parents do not have the emotional maturity to make baseball a fun game for children. He went on to say numerous things about how it was ruining what could be a great experience if only the parents and volunteers who coached kids would just back off and let kids have more control and fun during games.

His words filled me with encouragement and I shared the story with as many people as would listen. My youth league certification program was moving forward at full steam ahead and after a couple years I conducted more than a dozen clinics in the Wilmington area.

Because there were other CYO organizations throughout the country, I thought other directors would be interested in implementing similar programs. I organized a national conference and met with twenty-two other directors from around the country and spoke with them about the importance of having a certification program for volunteers and making youth sports fun for kids.

While trying to find effective speakers for the conference, I contacted a group out of Chicago that promoted sports equipment to youth leagues and athletes. There were called the Athletic Institute and I was impressed with the person they sent to represent their organization at our conference. As a matter of fact, we hit it off so well, that a week later I got a call from his boss, the president of the organization who, based on his employee's impression of me, offered me a job over the phone.

I assumed he'd heard about what I'd been doing with the certification programs and liked the idea. I thought this might be the way to get these ideas and programs to change youth sports nationwide.

"What will my job be?" I asked.

"You'll be representing our organization around the country."

While I was flattered, I was also frightened beyond belief. I really knew very little about the organization or what my job would be or if I would like doing it, but the bottom line was I was a father of six at that time, my wife was working part time just to keep food on the table and it was an opportunity to make more money.

Because the organization was located in Chicago, it would mean we'd have to uproot our six children and move half way across the country.

I wasn't sure of the decision, but I had a burning passion to make change in youth sports and I thought this might be the only chance I might ever have to get these ideas on a national stage. I just had to do it. When I explained how I felt about the opportunity to Mike, she amazed me once again by saying, "What ever we have to do to make it work...we'll do it!"

7

1973-1976
Chicago

My family, the eight of us, packed into a big Ford van and drove from Wilmington, Delaware to Chicago, Illinois in one long day filled with Motown music, I Spy games and breaking up arguments between the kids on issues ranging from who went to the bathroom last to which fast food restaurant had the best fast food. I had made one trip out a few weeks earlier to find a house and found one we could afford in a town not too far from Chicago called Munster, Indiana. The kids couldn't believe there was a place with such a crazy name.

The whole way there, I couldn't help feeling a little lost and overwhelmed. It was the fear of the unknown—a new part of the country, a new job, a new place to live.

"I really don't know," I said to Mike.

She knew exactly how I was feeling and said, "I think it's better to do things that make you a little afraid, than it is to not do them at all."

That made a lot of sense, but the way I was feeling reminded me of the day I was climbing up the side of the dog pit and not knowing which way to grasp or claw at the dirt.

My new job with The Athletic Institute was to promote sports. By definition, the company was a promotional arm of the sporting goods industry and its purpose was to expand the sales of sporting goods merchandise. I was hired to represent the company in the mid-west region, which meant lots of traveling and meeting with people who had any association with youth sports programs. While my new job description had little to do with youth sports directly, I knew my time would come to pitch the idea that making them more safe and fun would become of the most important contributions I could make.

At first, I loved the freedom and confidence the organization had in me. I was able to set my own schedule and make my own plans without a lot of interference from management. But after two months of visiting high schools and colleges pitching the importance of sports, I grew weary of the job. I felt like I was spinning my wheels. I believed in what I was doing, but didn't feel I was accomplishing anything. When my frustration boiled over one day, I walked into my boss's office and said, "I'm wasting your time and I'm wasting my time. I can do so much more than this."

To my amazement he calmly said, "So what would you think you could do that would be more productive?"

"I want to change things in youth sports in a way nobody else is even thinking about. There are so many things that could be done to fix the problems. Let me be the national director of youth sports and I'll start fixing things so kids have a better all-around experience no matter what sport they're playing," I said confidently.

"Why would making it more fun make any difference to the sports manufacturing companies? How's that going to help them? There aren't going to pay us just so little Jimmy has a better time in T-ball, Fred," he said sarcastically.

"Because in youth sports, I believe that thousands of young players are turned off by having the wrong people coaching them and when they quit, that's one less ball, bat and uniform the manufacturer is going to sell. I've got countless ideas to change the landscape for the better."

"Okay, you might be on to something there. I'll give you two months to show me your idea is going to be good for the sporting goods manufacturers and if it's not, then you'll be looking for another job."

Was I committing career suicide trying to change my own job description and role? I asked myself with a pit in my stomach and that feeling of desperation I couldn't seem to get rid of. I knew I had to do something spectacular to make him understand or else I was going to be jobless, trying to support a family of eight in a part of the country I knew nothing about.

Even though I was struggling to find my role and purpose at work, my family was settling in to the area nicely. After a couple months of living in Munster, the kids were enrolled in school and began to get interested in getting involved in youth sports in the area.

It didn't take long for me to see that youth sports here in Indiana were the same as they were back on the East Coast. When my son John decided he wanted to play Little League baseball I found out that to participate, you had to try out first. All the kids in the town who wanted to play on a team had to meet at a community park and demonstrate their skills. As they lined up, I heard the coaches call out the kid's names and then they were told to go out to the infield alone and catch pop ups and grounders as the coaches stood and assessed their individual skill levels.

I noticed one youngster, who was pacing and seemed scared to even be there. As his turn got closer, he began to cry and told his dad he wanted to go home. His dad yelled to him, "Don't you ever quit on me, boy. This is a man's game, now get in there!"

The boy then went out to the infield and the coach stood at home plate hitting him balls. Each ball that went by him ended up in the outfield. He couldn't pick up any of them. He obviously hadn't had a lot of training to prepare and was doomed from the start.

To my utter disgust, I heard one of the coaches say to another coach, "You got him on your team…good luck with that one."

"I ain't taking him," the other coach argued.

The boy heard the comments and ran off the field crying. I often wondered what his father said (or did) to him when they got home. I'd already witnessed many parents totally lose it when their children didn't live up to their expectations.

It was sad to see that kind of behavior again, but it was actually outside of organized sports where I may have had the most impactful and important experience that helped me form my philosophy for change.

We moved to a neighborhood that had a lot of children and during the summer months I watched my four boys run off to a nearby park to play baseball almost daily. They would get up seven days a week and talk about playing with the kids from across the street or around the block and debate about who would be on whose side. They would fight and argue and laugh about what was fair and who was better than whom. I heard about the games for a long time before I actually got in the car and drove down to watch one. I had to park a few blocks away from the field so they wouldn't notice an adult watching (which I was sure would ruin their fun).

What I witnessed was amazing. A dozen or so kids playing baseball on a dirty field with uncut grass and newspapers and rags for bases having the time of their lives. I'd never seen kids laugh and play like that before. Sure, they had disagreements, but they worked them out without needing an umpire. They may have been just keeping track of the score with a stick scratching numbers in the dirt, but you would've thought they were playing the World Series out there. The kids actually seemed to care about the game passionately and I saw them hugging and slapping backs after every run was scored. They seemed to be truly having fun and it really taught me something about how different sports for fun and organized sports were. Here, on a dirty field, there was no pressure to win. No parent or coach screaming at them about how important everything was. I got it now, why my son Eric said he didn't want to play Little League baseball anymore.

One morning that summer, my kids asked me if they could use some shovels and rakes to work on the field.

"What do you need all that stuff for?" I asked.

"We're playing a game against Highland tomorrow and we want the field to look good."

"Highland? Who's Highland?" I asked confused. I knew Highland was the town next to Munster, but what were they up to?

"Some of the kids from their neighborhood saw us playing down at the park and challenged us to a game and we want it all to look good so we're cutting the grass and laying in base lines and everything," my son David explained.

I couldn't believe that left on their own, kids could be so organized and productive without adult interference. I was impressed and said, "I can get you some bases and help you out with the field."

"We'll take the bases, but we can do the field by ourselves."

I knew that meant to back off and let them do things on their own.

About a week later, they played their big game with the rival town of Highland and for weeks I heard all about how they pulled off the win in the bottom of the ninth inning with an inside the park home run. No parents or coaches and they may have had one of the biggest and best moments involving sports in their young lives.

That experience made me more convinced than ever the ideas I had to improve youth sports could work. I believed it was something that just had to happen. I was now on a mission to make sports more fun for kids and I was going to do whatever I needed to do to make sure it happened.

Soon after the day I was given the order to produce some new way to expand and promote sports or I was going to lose my job, I began racking my brain for ideas. I knew what I wanted, but getting things to change on a large scale isn't easy. I lay in bed at night thinking and asking myself over and over, *What can I do to make this happen?*

Then an idea came and with it a tactic I was sure would work. I'd thought back to my days at the YMCA and coaching the rag-tag football team, and especially the days at the CYO. *I wonder if the heads of the many youth sports organizations and the sporting goods manufacturers in America had ever met to discuss the problems in youth sports face-to-face?* That was it and I knew what I had to do to make it work.

I couldn't wait to tell my boss about an idea to invite the heads of every youth sport organization from Little League Baseball to Pop Warner Football to a national conference. I would put together a blockbuster agenda and it would be the first time in history it had ever been done.

The next morning when I got to work, I asked the boss if we could meet. When I told him my idea, he replied, "That has got to be the dumbest idea I have ever heard...do you really think that all these organizations who deal with virtually the same kids day in and day out would want to sit in the same room with one another?"

I said, "Absolutely, I think they would and I know exactly what you're going to tell them when you're there."

"Me?!" he said raising his voice in disbelief.

"Yes, you. This is my tactic and I'm sure it will work. I want you to introduce the program and ask them all what are the biggest problems they face. You need to get them to recognize they all have the same problems and then I'll come in and offer the many ideas I have for the solutions. This has never been done before and could be an historic event!"

He smiled and countered by saying, "I'll give it one shot, but like I said before, if this doesn't work it will be your swan song for the Institute. You'll be out of job here."

I sent letters of invitation to 27 youth sports organization directors and some leaders in the sporting goods manufacturing industry across the country and made arrangements for the facility we'd use for the conference. To my relief and surprise, 26 replied they would attend. I couldn't wait to tell the boss and when I did, I could see in his eyes he had developed a new bit of confidence in me.

On the day of the event, my boss delivered the introduction speech I prepared for him and it went over so well the group stood with applause and smiles of encouragement. Then, I took over the room with, "Now that we all agree that we have some serious problems to deal with, are we just going to put our heads in the sand and hope they go away?"

It was the beginning of a renaissance in youth sports. All those who attended agreed that bad coaches and overzealous parents were huge headaches for organizations, yet not one of them thought there was a solution.

One of the many ideas I suggested was the same thing that I'd instituted back at the CYO in Wilmington—a mandated training program forcing coaches to learn how to be better coaches and role models to the kids. I also spoke of the importance of having parents understand this was supposed to be fun for kids – not a pressure-filled event where they could relive their childhoods. I suggested an educational program for parents requiring them know their role and act accordingly at games. And I suggested that recreational directors be educated in first aid to ensure kids had a safe and positive experience while playing sports at their facilities.

The response from many of these organizational leaders was that even though they agreed changes had to be made for the better, most were afraid to mandate anything for fear of losing the volunteers who made up the league.

"You are the ones that have identified the problems," I said, "Don't you think we should do something for the kid's sake?"

I once again had to give in a little to the fears of change many had, but the seeds for change were planted and the conference went off without a hitch. During the conference I suggested we form the National Organization of Youth Sports Directors and that we'd meet annually to discuss the issues. Almost every organization agreed to take part.

I was standing next to my boss when the president of one of the sporting goods organizations approached and said, "You know, I've got to tell you a story. When I was a kid, I saw everything you brought up at this conference—the abusive coaches and screaming parents. I have to admit I even feel guilt to this day over the way I pushed and treated my own kids when they were playing sports and I feel awful about it. I want you to know I'm proud to be part of this and I'll do what ever it takes to help you folks out."

My boss couldn't have been happier with the outcome of the event. The Athletic Institute was now a name and a force in organized youth sports across America and the sporting goods manufacturers associations (our employers) were on board one hundred percent.

Flying back to Chicago I was on cloud nine. Filled with a great sense of accomplishment and I was back in very good standing at the Institute. However, a few months later, something very bad happened at the Institute—my boss retired his position and there was a significant change at the top.

After all the work I'd done to win my old boss over, I had to start all over again with a new one…and this one was as bad as bosses can be. A couple of hours after being introduced, he summoned me into his office and asked me to lay out what my responsibilities were.

"I'm the National Director of Youth Sports and my role is to help youth sports organizations become more focused on making organized sports fun, safe and an overall more positive experience," I told him.

I could tell from his expression he wasn't impressed with what I was telling him.

And then he said, "Let me make something perfectly clear to you. I come from the sports industry and what the sports industry is about is making money. We aren't in the business of making people happy. We are in the business of getting more young athletes to buy more equipment. Period. End of story. Tell me how you are gonna prove to me that what you are doing actually works."

"That would require a lot of time and research," I explained.

"Not going to happen then!"

It was his way of telling me two things—my role was changing and he was the boss. He didn't care how, he wanted the numbers of participants up.

I began to explain how my ideas could do just that, but he interrupted and said, "Too slow. How can you prove what you are saying? We need new ideas to bring up the numbers faster!"

The words from the new boss left an ugly feeling in my stomach and even after all the work I'd done, I was left feeling the opportunity to grow my ideas and programs here was disappearing.

It had been two and a half years since we left Wilmington, Delaware, and life in the Midwest was much different than being on the East Coast. The winters were as harsh as winters could get, with five months of the year typically below freezing. Even though the job paid a lot more than back at the CYO, I was still supporting six kids and it wasn't always easy to keep food on the table.

Mike not only had to make things work on a tight budget, but she would also work seasonal, part-time jobs to insure we'd have money for Christmas. I knew she wasn't a big fan of the cold weather and she yearned for the day we could move back to the East Coast, but that didn't appear to be in the picture.

Fortunately, to my surprise and relief, not long after the new boss arrived, I began hearing rumors the Athletic Institute was moving and to a place nobody expected.

8

1976-1980
The Gamble

In the spring of 1976, the new president of the Athletic Institute announced they were moving the organization to West Palm Beach, Florida. I couldn't wait to tell Mike and the kids the news.

After three very cold and harsh winters, living near the ocean among palm trees in the sunshine seemed too good to be true. It was like telling them the rest of their lives would be a sunny vacation. They were all thrilled and only wanted to know one thing, "When are we leaving?"

Just like we did a few years earlier, we hopped in the same van and headed south for a new life. But my role with the Athletic Institute was turning into something that was anything but sunny. The new president, my boss, was a tyrant. He ran the organization from a fear basis. To a person, everyone on the staff either feared or hated him. For me, it was a little bit of both.

One day he called me into his office and proceeded to tell me he didn't like what I was doing and hadn't for a long time. He said I was wasting his time. At this point, I'd worked for the Institute more than five years. I'd represented it well at conferences and meetings all over the United States and even Germany and this man was still talking down to me. It immediately took me back to my days in the seminary when the bully would talk to me in threatening tones.

When he finished, I said, "You can think what you want, sir, but let me tell you, I'm tired of the way you talk to me. I'm not taking it any more," and stormed out of his office. I felt sure I was going to be fired and didn't even care. It didn't happen though, and the next day he simply avoided me.

I was tired of being treated like that and weary of working with supervisors who would only give me limited control. I dreamed of starting an organization on my own that would create a certification program for youth coaches, but with the news that Mike was pregnant with our seventh child, I was too afraid to make the leap. I talked with her almost on a daily basis about the idea, but we both knew we couldn't afford to do it. However, as always, she told me whatever I decided to do, she would back me up and do whatever she could to make it a success.

She wasn't the only person I'd talked with about quitting and starting out on my own, and somehow it got back to my boss. For the first time in quite a while, he asked me to join him for lunch.

"So what's this, you're thinking about leaving us?" he asked.

Startled, I said, "Yes, I don't have much of a plan yet, but yes, I'm looking into moving on and out on my own."

"You are leaving us....I'm not happy about this at all," he said in an intimidating way.

Without a real plan, without a lot of confidence in what I was doing, I said, "Yes, I'm quitting." I had become very friendly with many of the executive members in the sporting goods industry. The boss was offended by this because these people were in fact his bosses. When I announced to him I was leaving he feared I would tell the members it was because of him. He had no idea what I was going to do and hoped I just might fade away after a few months. He was wrong.

I went back to my office and packed it up that afternoon. When I left work that day I began to panic. Seven mouths to feed, a mortgage and now I was trying to take on starting my own organization with minimal start-up cash. To try and give myself a boost of confidence, I called my son John's baseball coach to tell him of my idea to start a national organization to create better coaches, administrators, parents and experiences for the kids participating. His name was Phil, and I considered him a fairly knowledgeable and rational guy and good coach. When I told him the idea about the organization, he gave me a very sobering opinion.

"Fred, there is not one person out there in America that wouldn't think this is a great idea, but the problem is nobody has the time for something like this in their lives. They are already volunteering a lot of their time just coaching."

I was temporarily devastated by his words, but in spite of his opinion, I had nowhere else to go but forward. It was a little like being back in that dog pit. I had no other options but react and quickly.

Along with Mike's help, we put together a manual for coaches that included everything you needed to know about coaching. Fortunately, from my years of learning about so many problems, I had lots of ideas as to what could be important to create a change in the culture of coaching. I solicited opinions from professionals and did extensive research to incorporate ideas involving the psychological aspects of coaching, first aid and safety, and positive coaching techniques.

Mike and I, with the help of our kids, collated the manuals and put them into binders. I created a name for our organization, the National Youth Sports Coaches Association. We were off and running…until the next day. Mike, acting as secretary, answered the phone and began by saying, "Are you sure?"

She hung up the phone and said the most gut-wrenching words a man with the weight of the world on his chest can hear, "We're overdrawn!"

Talk about life smacking you in the face. It was so scary I even called my mother for help. Somehow through the years, she'd save and put money aside for an emergency and was able to help.

Members of three major Sporting Goods Company agreeing to donate $36,000 to start the National Youth Sports Coaches Association

Over 8000 pounds of sports equipment has been shipped to developing countries around the world.

When you are desperate you can get pretty creative. I remember telling Mike there was still a chance to make everything work, "The reason they were so unhappy when I left the Athletic Institute was that I'd formed a lot of relationships and connections with the important people of major sporting goods manufacturers, and their annual sports product show in New York City is only a week away. If I go there and pitch this idea, one of them will bite."

"But you don't work for them anymore. How can you show up uninvited?" she said.

"I guess we'll find out."

Before I left, I called many of the presidents from the sporting goods companies. I had formed friendly relationships with most of them and was on a first name basis. They all agreed to meet with me to discuss my idea of going national with the training programs.

By this time, my old boss was getting word I was trying to get the organization off the ground. The idea for it which he called the most harebrained he'd ever heard. Either way, I knew he would not like the idea of me showing up to talk with the folks from the manufacturers groups, so when I got there I tried to be as invisible as possible.

As I walked in, an old friend who was editor of one of the sports industry magazines was there and I told him about the project immediately.

"You've got to be shitting me. I love it," he said.

He was encouraging, but warned me that if my boss, the guy who helped put on the event and sponsor it, saw me, he would probably have me removed on sight.

After a couple hours, I'd quietly met individually with the presidents of Puma, MacGregor and Spanjian sporting goods and told them each about my idea, and that without their help, I would never be able to get it off the ground.

I said to each of them, sounding perhaps as if I were pleading for my life, "Gentlemen, this is either the first day or the last day of my newly founded organization."

I showed them the manuals I'd created and prayed they wouldn't think I was off my rocker or that the idea was "harebrained." To my surprise they were all enthusiastic and receptive to the idea.

By the end of the day I had $36,000 pledged to go toward my new organization. As I stood there talking with one of sporting goods representatives, I heard a voice from someone peering in from a doorway, "Is Fred Engh in here?"

My heart dropped as I knew my time was up and my goose was cooked. I thought my boss had found me, but it was only that magazine editor who'd already heard of my success in convincing these men to help my fledgling organization. He simply wanted to get us together for a group shot for the cover of his next magazine.

Minutes later, I stood there in the hall outside the venue having my picture taken with three prominent sporting goods presidents as they presented me checks and words of encouragement. My former boss watched from across the hall with a disgusted look on his face.

When I finally left the building, I rushed to the nearest phone booth to tell Mike the news: "We did it. We did it. We have support. We are off to the races. We can get an office now!"

"Unbelievable. I knew you could do it," she said.

She was in shock for a moment and then said how happy she was to know that we could move forward with the organization. As I rode home on the plane, I was still in disbelief the plan worked. I was in awe of how lucky I was that I wasn't turned down. It could have just as easily gone the other way.

"Would my luck continue? Will I be able to make this vision a reality?" I wondered. Then I thought of everything I'd done leading up to this moment—the struggles, the hurdles, the dogs, the seminary. I'd overcome a lot in my life and at that moment it felt as if it were just beginning.

Epilogue

By Greg Bach

Not long after that trip to New York, the organization took off and, after 33 years, Fred Engh remains the President and CEO of the National and International Alliance for Youth Sports.

Fred's burning passion to help children throughout the world learn about the life lessons he gained from sports has never wavered and "vision, passion and commitment" are the tenants that have guided him throughout life. Above it all he says, "But few people have been as lucky as me."

In 1983, many youth league organizations revolted when Fred suggested all youth sports groups were doing a disservice to children by not having volunteers trained and held accountable for their behavior. Little League Baseball's president sent a letter to all of its affiliates throughout the world suggesting they have nothing to do with Fred and his organization. He stated that what Fred was doing to require coaches to be formally trained by his organization would destroy Little League.

By 1993, the organization was growing by leaps and bounds and had almost one million coaches trained under the NYSCA banner. Because coaches were only a part of the problem facing youth sports, the organization decided to broaden the outreach by changing the name to the National Alliance for Youth Sports (NAYS). The expanded training programs educate parents on their important role as well as youth league directors and officials. A youth sports development division was created to help children gain the necessary skills and confidence needed before being forced out onto ball fields, rinks and courts without any understanding of what would be required for them to have fun.

In 1998 the organization felt a need to provide communities with written guidelines and recommendations for allocating facilities to parent–run youth sports programs. More than 40 youth sports leaders from around the country attended and developed the now available *Recommendations for Youth Sports* manual.

In 2000, under Fred's leadership, NAYS organized the first-ever National Conference on Safety in Youth Baseball. Recently, it had been announced that 7 children had died as the result of being struck by a baseball. In addition, other injuries were occurring, thus the need to examine ways to prevent these occurrences. Because of the many incidents, one youth league organization in Jupiter, Florida announced it would make it mandatory for all parents to attend the NAYS's parent education program before their child was allowed to participate. This incident drew national attention and once again, Fred appeared on programs such as *Good Morning America, The Today Show, ESPN's Outside the Lines* and a host of radio and news print media reports.

In 2004, because of Fred's undying desire to help ALL children around the world, the International Alliance for Youth Sports (IAYS) was born and today more than 16 developing countries have received training and sports equipment to initiate sustainable sports programs for children. One of his greatest achievements has been a formal partnership with Children International, a child sponsorship organization. Fred's signature program, Game On! Youth Sports, gives more than 300,000 children the opportunity to play sports through the Children International partnership. With the success of the Game On! Program with Children International, other countries began to be included in the expansion of the program. In particular, the country of Haiti where IAYS has teamed up with a local nonprofit Haiti organization called Global Haitian Advancement through

Education and Sports. More than 150 boxes of sports equipment have been sent to the hurricane and earthquake ravaged country.

Grown out of his love for the game of golf and his experience of playing on an all-African-American team in college, Fred created a program called Hook A Kid On Golf in 2002. The program gives the opportunity for those less likely to experience the game of golf the opportunity to learn all aspects of the game at an early age. To date, more than 75,000 young people have graduated from the program.

Personal tragedy struck when Fred's grandson, Sammy, age 9, died in a tragic accident in 2003 by falling through the ice at, ironically, his local recreation department. Fred created the Sammy Wilkinson Memorial Foundation that has raised close to $250,000 to help support the International mission of the Alliance. Through the program's Global Gear Drive, it has shipped almost 15,000 pounds of sports equipment to developing countries around the world as well as to local and national programs in need.

Some of Fred's personal achievements over the years include the following:

- 2007: Invited speaker at the pre-Olympic Symposium on Sports
- 2009: Named one of America's top 100 sports educators
- 2010: Invited to India where he spoke before 20,000 people about the value of sports in the lives of children
- 2011: Signed a partnership with the International Alliance for Youth Sports and the Peace Corps
- 2011: Invited speaker at the Doha, Qatar worldwide forum on sports

In addition to all of the above, Fred's talents go well beyond sports. He is the author of, *Why Johnny Hates Sports* which chronicles the problems in sports for children and how we can change the landscape.

Few people have the courage to follow their dreams and the passion to make them come true no matter how high the odds are stacked against them. But Fred Engh is unique, a true visionary, one who has dedicated his life to making a difference in the lives of children – all through the amazing power of sports. From humble beginnings to creating a global organization that has forever altered the youth sports landscape for the better, his remarkable story is truly one of fortitude, determination, perseverance and belief.

Greg Bach is the author of *Coaching Youth Sports for Dummies Series*.

Acknowledgments

I'm sure no book has ever been written without the help of people around you who are willing to give their experienced advice. The below are some of those people.

Greg Bach. It's always nice knowing that sitting two doors down from your office is one of the most prolific writers I know. Greg has pumped out more stories and books than anyone I know. I've called on him so many times for his advice I'm sure he's tired of hearing his phone buzz knowing it was me for one more question.

Jeri Engh. If the last name sounds familiar it's because Jeri is my sister-in-law. I've leaned on Jeri for her advice because of her extensive background as a writer and editor.

Rick Robinson. Rick has been a friend for the past 30 years. He's an award winning author and his encouragement, throughout the process of writing this book, is what made it all happen.

Timeline

1981

- Twenty-one coaches participate in the first-ever NYSCA clinic in West Palm Beach, Fla.

1982

- Stokely-Van Camp, Inc., maker of Gatorade, sponsors NYSCA, along with McGregor Sporting Goods, Spanjian Sportswear and Puma USA.

1983

- NYSCA's first training tape debuts featuring Dr. Richard Magill.

1984

- *Youth Sport Coach* becomes the official publication of NYSCA.

1985

- DeKalb County (Georgia) becomes the first to mandate the NYSCA program for its coaches.

1986

- NYSCA's state directors gather for the first time in West Palm Beach to discuss implementing the program in their state.

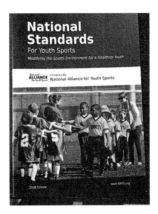

1987

- The National Standards for Youth Sports are created

1989

- NYSCA's first-ever national conference, featuring U.S. Olympic Committee Executive Director Aaron Pittenger as keynote speaker, takes place in Orlando, Fla.

1990

- PGA golf professional Bob Murphy becomes the national spokesperson for *Hook A Kid on Golf*

- Detroit Piston great Isiah Thomas delivers the keynote address at NYSCA's second annual conference. He's joined by Major Leaguer George Foster, Olympian Bob Beamon and the NFL's Carl Eller and Pat McInally.

- The United States Golf Association approves a $90,000 challenge grant to NAYS for the implementation of *Hook A Kid On Golf* nationwide. Eighteen communities participate in the first-year pilot program.

1991

- The National Summit For Safety In Youth Baseball and Softball is held in Orlando.

1992

- *The Sportsmanship in Youth Sports Summit* is held in San Antonio, Texas.

1993

- *Hook A Kid On Golf* receives the prestigious Golf Digest Junior Development Award.

1994

- NYSCA evolves into

- Twenty-four youngsters and their parents are all smiles as they throw, catch and kick Koosh balls while participating in the first Start Smart Sports Development Program in Naples, Fla.

- *Hook A Kid On Golf* receives the PGA Tour's prestigious Card Walker Award for the outstanding contributions it has made to junior golf.

- Oddz On, the creators of the Koosh ball, award $20,000 to help develop the *Start Smart Sports* Development program.

- The Callaway Golf Foundation donates $50,000 to help create the Community Sharing Grants program to support local *Hook A Kid On Golf* programs.

1995

• Baumholder, Germany, is the site of the first *Hook A Kid On Golf* clinic held on European soil.

1996

• The Alliance launches its website at www.nays.org.

• Bob King, director of Bradley County Parks & Recreation in Cleveland, Tennessee, certifies NYSCA's one-millionth coach. King receives a special letter of recognition from President Clinton.

• A total of 1,040 officials go through the National Youth Sports Officials Association during its first year of existence.

1997

• *Start Smart* is implemented at youth centers on U.S. Air Bases throughout Europe.

• Dateline NBC visits Alliance headquarters and interviews Fred Engh.

• The USGA Foundation commits $100,000 per year to *Hook A Kid On Golf* as part of its *For The Good Of The Game* initiative.

1998

• The Troy Parks and Recreation Department in Michigan hosts the first *Start Smart Baseball* program.

- The doors to *Hook A Kid On Golf*'s first-ever state office open in Illinois. Jerry Rich and Don Springer create the *Hook A Kid On Golf* of Illinois Foundation with the help of the first Bob Murphy Pro-Am at Rich Harvest Farms in Sugar Grove, Ill. Over $500,000 is raised to support the program regionally.

1999

- *Why Johnny Hates Sports,* written by Alliance President Fred Engh, hits bookstores nationwide.

- More than 100 youngsters from 16 cities nationwide arrive in Peoria, Illinois, for the first *Hook A Kid On Golf Traditions of Golf Challenge*.

2000

- The Jupiter-Tequesta Athletic Association becomes the first organization in the country to make the Parents Association for Youth Sports program mandatory. More than 2,000 parents file into Roger Dean Stadium for the first mandatory session, which is covered by NBC Nightly News, ABC World News Tonight, the CBS Evening News, ESPN, Sports Illustrated and CNN.

- NFL Hall of Fame coach Don Shula presents the first-ever Excellence in Youth Sports Awards at the annual Athletic Business Conference.

- The National Youth Sports Administrators Association program is launched for league presidents, board members and other volunteer administrators.

2001

- Febreze, a Proctor and Gamble product, sponsors the Time Out! For Better Sports For Kids booklet and Olympic gold medalist Marion Jones serves as national spokesperson.

- The National Summit on Raising Community Standards in Children's Sports is held in Chicago.

- Start Smart Golf debuts at the Wilton Family YMCA in Conn.

2002

- The *Recommendations for Communities,* which were established from the National Summit on Raising Community Standards in

- Children's Sports, are released.

- More than 300 delegates convene in San Antonio, Texas, for the first-ever International Youth Sports Congress. Award-winning writer Lester Munson of *Sports Illustrated* delivers the keynote address.

- Franklin becomes the official manufacturer of *Start Smart Sports Development* products.

- Start Smart Basketball debuts at Peoria Community Services in Ariz.

2003

- *Time Out!* kids Tammy and Sammy created.

- The International Alliance For Youth Sports is formed.

- Parents have the opportunity to go through the Parents Association for Youth Sports program from the comfort of home thanks to the unveiling of the on-line program.

- The first International Summit on Youth Sports is held in Atlanta, Georgia.

- Hook A Kid On Golf becomes an official partner with the Ladies Professional Golf Association's LPGA – USGA Girls Golf program.

2004

- The two-millionth coach is trained by NYSCA.

- Dr. Thomas Tutko receives first-ever Heisman Trophy Foundation/NAYS Youth Sports Achievement Award.

- U.S. Disabled Athletes Fund and Alliance release "Coaching Adaptive Sports" program.

2005

- High-ranking sports officials from more than a dozen countries throughout the Caribbean, as well as Mexico and Zambia, gather in Roseau, Dominica, for the first-ever Caribbean Conference on Children's Sports.

- *SportingKid* magazine becomes the official member publication of the Alliance.

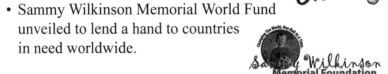

- *Game On! Youth Sports*, a first-of-its-kind approach that created opportunities for children to participate in healthy physical activities that otherwise wouldn't have the opportunity to do so, is launched in Dominica.

- NYSCA unveils online training programs to make clinics more accessible for coaches.

- Sammy Wilkinson Memorial World Fund unveiled to lend a hand to countries in need worldwide.

- Start Smart Football debuts at the Tyndall Air Force Base Youth Center in Fla.

2006

- Delegates throughout Africa take part in the first-ever Game On! African Summit in Lusaka, Zambia.

- Alliance releases background check guidelines to assist leagues based on findings from a special session on background screening held during the International Youth Sports Congress in Denver.

- Baseball great Cal Ripken, Jr. named official spokesperson for Game On! Youth Sports.

- International Alliance For Youth Sports establishes office in Queretaro, Mexico.

- Alliance celebrates its 25th anniversary in Washington, D.C., during the annual International Youth Sports Congress.

2007

- The Youth Sports Congress is held in conjunction with the Athletic Business Conference in Orlando, Fla.

- The Supreme Council for Sport in Africa (SCSA) signs Memorandum of Understanding with IAYS to implement Game On! Youth Sports programs throughout Africa.

2008

- The National Standards for Youth Sports are reviewed and updated by over 200 youth sports professionals in San Antonio, Texas.

- The first ever NAYS Youth Sports Study was conducted with the results featured in *SportingKid* magazine.

2009

- NYSCA members are given access to a personalized online page.

- NYSCA unveils its Coach Ratings Tool.

- The NAYS Chapter Management system is created allowing chapters instant access to training, background check and evaluation information on their members.

2010

- The Accountability Policies and Procedures for NYSCA members is released to track coach incidents through NAYS chapters.

- The NYSCA Coach Training program is re-released that includes Mike Krzyzewski, Vivian Stringer, John Harbaugh and many others.

- IAYS introduces its ONE WORLD. ONE TEAM. initiative to help provide selected communities with educational support and equipment through donated funds.

- IAYS teams up with Sports4HOPE to provide sports equipment for approximately 300 children in war-torn regions of the Eastern Democratic Republic of Congo.

- IAYS signs agreement with the General Direction for Physical Education (DIGEF), a Guatemalan government agency, to bring sports to children throughout Guatemala through its Game On! Youth Sports program.

- More than 20,000 people are on hand for the unveiling of the Game On! Youth Sports program in India.

2011

- *The Ready, Set, RUN!* program was created.

- IAYS and the Peace Corps formed a new partnership.

- IAYS works with Peace Corps volunteers stationed in Totonicapan, Guatemala.

- Children International and IAYS conduct 10-day training in Guadalajara, Mexico featuring representatives from nine agencies of Children International throughout Mexico, Guatemala, Dominican Republic, Colombia, Honduras and Chile.

- IAYS releases series of educational resources designed to help communities jumpstart or improve their current youth sports programming at school or within their community.

- NAYS Founder Fred Engh featured on Golf Channel's *Golf Central* highlighting his life, including being the only Caucasian golfer on the golf team at the historically all-black Maryland State College in the early 1960s.

2012

- A new NYSCA Online area was unveiled to volunteer coaches.

- Alliance releases updated background check guidelines to assist leagues based on findings from screening session held during the Youth Sports Congress in Orlando.

- A new NYSAA Online area was unveiled to volunteer administrators.

- The Global Gear Drive sent much-needed sports gear to the New Orleans Recreation Department (NORD) Foundation as part of a special initiative to provide long-term support to the foundation's youth sports programs.

- The Global Gear Drive provides sports equipment to the Association to Benefit Children in New York City.

2013

- The NYSCA Select program was created for elite and traveling coaches.

- Alliance unveils a new Concussion and Bullying Prevention Training programs for volunteer coaches and parents. Both programs are offered at no cost.

- A new PAYS Online area was unveiled for parents.

2014

- Free Concussion and Bullying Prevention Training programs were created for non-members.

- A new NYSOA Online area was unveiled for volunteer officials and referees. In addition a new CYSA Online area was unveiled for professional administrators.

- The Sports Parent Pledge was created to promote positivity and have parents advocate for good sportsmanship in youth sports.

- NAYS unveils a new Prevention Against Abuse Training program for coaches and parents.

- NAYS launches a new video web series called Game Changers featuring current and former professional coaches and players.

- The Kenya Sports Foundation (KESOFO), a sporting nongovernmental organization based in Eldoret, Kenya received certification to become an official Game On! Youth Sports organization.

2015

- Game On! Youth Sports joins with Global Haitian Advancement in Education and Sports organization in Haiti. IAYS pledges 105 boxes of sports uniforms and equipment.